Die Hard, Aby!

Die Hard, Aby!

Abraham Bevistein, a boy
soldier shot to encourage
the others

by

David Lister

Pen & Sword
MILITARY

First published in Great Britain in 2005 by
Pen & Sword Military
an imprint of
Pen & Sword Books Ltd
47 Church Street
Barnsley
South Yorkshire
S70 2AS

ISBN 1 84415 137 9

A CIP catalogue record for this book is
available from the British Library

Typeset in 11/13 Sabon by
Kirsten Barber, Leeds, West Yorkshire

Printed and bound by
CPI UK

For a complete list of Pen & Sword titles please contact
PEN & SWORD BOOKS LIMITED
47 Church Street, Barnsley, South Yorkshire, S70 2AS, England
E-mail: enquiries@pen-and-sword.co.uk
Website: www.pen-and-sword.co.uk

To the memory of A.B.

and

for Betty and Ralph Jacobs

Contents

Preface

It is almost as if the case of the First World War British and Commonwealth soldiers who were shot at dawn is a recurring, national itch that requires scratching at frequent intervals. Possibly a nagging feeling by some that justice has not been done, that feeling striking at the heart of a people who like to see fair play. Others may just wish the subject would fade away, and pretty much feel that justice was done in the first place.

There are several books that address the issue but even before the first of them had been conceived, interest in the subject bubbled away under the surface from a time well before the cessation of hostilities in 1919.

Drawing on questions in the House, the rumours and accusations and other sources that alluded to the soldiers, who were to the consternation of successive governments proving to be the unquiet dead who would not be silenced, *The Thin Yellow Line* was published in 1974. Its author, William Moore, had to make as good a job of it as possible without recourse to official court martial papers, for these had been closed to the public, and marked 'not for release' until the expiration of one hundred years.

Ten years later, Anthony Babington's *For the Sake of Example* was the first book published by an author who had been allowed to see the papers, still not yet within the public domain. Seventy-five years after the executions, the government relenting to public pressure, the War Office documents were released earlier than first intended, thus enabling more research. At this time, another work, *Shot at Dawn* by Julian Putkowski and Julian Sykes was published. This was the first book to report on a detailed study of the individual cases, and also the first where those executed were named within the body of the work as opposed to within a table or index.

All these books lean towards the injustice of the situation, with the latter making a strong case for the pardoning of all those executed for disciplinary offences, such as desertion or sleeping at post. One of the most recent works on the subject was published in 2001 and is the well researched but unusually unsympathetic *Blindfold and Alone* by Cathryn Corns and John Hughes-Wilson. This book takes the general stance that the executions were, for the most part, properly carried out and probably necessary.

For God's Sake Shoot Straight (recently published under the new title *Death for Desertion*) by Leonard Sellers tells the story of Sub Lieutenant Edwin Dyett, one of only two officers shot for military offences during the First World War.

It is suggested that *Die Hard, Aby!* follows a logical sequence, trailing in the wake of the above mentioned publications. William Moore brought the issue of the executions to the wider public for the first time. Anthony Babington examined the case in more depth. The two Julians gave us details, linked names to stories and raised a strong call for pardons. Cathryn Corns and John Hughes-Wilson presented a detailed pro-establishment account, and Leonard Sellers' book is the story of an executed officer. *Die Hard, Aby!* similarly seeks to examine the story of the enlisted men and in particular Abraham Bevistein, who like an estimated 15 per cent of all fighting men within the New Army, had signed up as a soldier, under age.

This work seeks to tell his whole story. Where was he born? Where did he grow up? What influences were at work during his short life, and what chain of events brought him to his fate? Abraham was a very ordinary boy amongst the hundreds of thousands of ordinary boys and men who died in the trenches and whose lives leave not even a footnote on the pages of history. A name on a stone or a memorial panel – but no more than that. This work will tell of little twists of fate that caused Abraham's name to become more than an anonymous line in a Role of Honour. It will record how he has been mentioned in Hansard on occasions spanning in excess of seventy years and how his story exemplifies an injustice that has been allowed to endure for far too long.

This story is not that of the 306 men executed for military offences; it is that of one boy who suffered that end, of Abraham Bevistein, who served under the name 'Harris' and whose gravestone bears the name spelt incorrectly as 'Beverstein'. The author fully acknowledges he is not immune to bias, but states that he will make all conscious efforts to avoid personal views from taking control of the processes of recording Abraham's footnote in history.

Much of the work speaks of Abraham's times and the setting for his life, especially in the early chapters. After the passage of years, there is little to be found in records and archives of the life of one boy who grew up in a poor part of London. That does not mean to say there is nothing at all, and such as is available serves well to root him in time and location. We follow Abraham from the Russian annexed land of his birth, across Europe and the North Sea and into a new land for which he chose to fight, and for which he ultimately died. We learn a little of his school life, the regiment he joined and of the events that brought him to his untimely death. During our journey we will meet people whose faces Abraham may well have known, or who somehow touch upon his story. Finally we explore how the sad case of an executed boy was taken up in Parliament and how letters from the front, scribbled on scraps of paper, were brought to the attention of the nation.

At the end of the book it will be for the reader to decide whether Abraham Bevistein has been afforded fair justice from the country for which he died – even after all these years.

Acknowledgements

Aby has led me to some amazing places since I started to research his life and times. It all came about when my son was assigned to complete a school project about Field Marshal Douglas Haig. Knowing a little about those who were shot at dawn, I thought he would get a paragraph or two from the subject. Then we discovered Aby. My son's project was soon completed, but Aby kept niggling me. 'Find out more about me!' he seemed to say. 'But I'm not going to make it easy!' he would add with a mischievous grin.

My hope for the future is that Aby's story will come to be known as widely as possible, which is some compensation for the stigma still attached to his name, that successive governments, to their great shame and dishonour, will probably never lift. Maybe there are dusty diaries somewhere or old photo albums where more details of Aby's life might be hidden. Perhaps the missing letters will one day turn up. Stranger things have happened.

In the eighteen months or so it has taken me to research and write up an account of his life, I have been fortunate to find help at almost every turn, whether it be from patient archivists at the London Metropolitan Archives, Public Record Office staff or the National Army Museum, to individuals who have given their time and knowledge to help Aby's story come to light. I have learnt many things during the journey, not least of which is to keep better tabs on my sources. I have quoted as many of them as I can in the 'Sources and Bibliography' but there have been so many, especially on the Internet, that the list is woefully inadequate.

My first acknowledgement must be to the many unsung contributors to the global body of information that is the World Wide Web. Dipping into this staggeringly vast mass of information has saved me time immeasurable and has guided me to sources and archives of which I would never otherwise have heard.

These acknowledgements would be incomplete without the mention of certain individuals. The first that must be cited is George Coppard, whose work I have quoted often in *Die Hard, Aby!* He was in the same division as Aby, and often their respective battalions were working in close proximity. To anyone who wants to hear more first hand accounts of a soldier who served in the same locations as Aby, I commend his book, *With a Machine Gun to Cambrai*, which at the time of writing, is still in print and available from Cassell Military Paperbacks.

I would like to thank John Hipkin for all his hard work and dedication to the cause of the 306 men and boys executed for military offences. A 'pen and paper' man, he co-ordinates the campaign for pardons without such modern necessities as a computer. I thank him for putting me in touch with many people who have been able to point me in the right direction or guide me away from dead-ends. I am also grateful to Anne Mary Jayes who spoke to me of her father's pain at having to command a firing party to shoot 'a poor frightened boy'. Thanks also to author Richard van Emden for guiding me to some Hansard references concerning Aby that I had previously overlooked.

Betty Jacobs is Aby's only surviving niece and I would like to thank her for sharing her East End memories and for the excellent photograph of Aby with his mother, father and sister Kate on the occasion of his bar mitzvah. Betty has been very encouraging throughout this project, and I only hope the work meets expectation. Thanks also to Hew Strachen for answering my query concerning the matter of cocaine being given to men at the front. Thank you Sam Seager, for directing me towards the on-line facility for searching the registers of The Poor Jews' Shelter, and to other resources within the PRO.

Thanks to my wife Marion, for reading endless reams of first draft sections, and doing more than her share of the domestic chores while I scribble away or visit dusty archives. Also to the patience of my sons, Michael and Nathan.

A little of Aby's story was included in a Channel 4 dramatized documentary and I would like to thank Testimony Films – especially executive producer Steve Humphries and producer/director Neil Rawles – for the care they took to get the story as close to reality as dramatic interpretation would allow. And thank you to actor Josh Maguire who portrayed Aby. I was able to observe much of his work from behind the camera and on the lip of the trench, and I was moved by his acting and impressed by his care to 'get it right'. The finished work, *Britain's Boy Soldiers,* was first shown in June 2004 and received much critical acclaim, Aby's story especially, catching public interest. Many thanks indeed to Lizi Cosslett of Testimony Films for her successful efforts to help me secure use of some of the photos included in *Die Hard, Aby!,* and for a thousand and one other contributions that have helped Aby's story towards the light of day. Thanks also to photographer Simon Rawles for his kind permission to use the two excellent shots of Aby as portrayed by Josh Maguire.

I am very grateful to Brigadier Henry Wilson and the staff at Pen & Sword Books for seeing the potential in Aby's story, and especially to Kirsten Barber for knocking the rough edges off my work and for unravelling my convoluted sentences.

My final and most heartfelt acknowledgement must go to Tommy. Private Tommy Atkins. RSM Tommy Atkins. Even Lieutenant Thomas Atkins. In all his ranks, in all his roles, in all his many guises.

Glossary

ADC	Aide de Campe
APM	Assistant Provost Marshal – usually of Lieutenant Colonel Rank
ASC	Army Service Corps
Blighty	Home (Britain)
Blighty one	A wound sufficiently serious for the recipient to be shipped home, but not life threatening or permanently debilitating
CB	Commander of the British Empire
CCS	Casualty Clearing Station
CMG	Commander of the Order of St Michael and St George
CO	Commanding Officer
Count coup	From a Native American expression; to strike at the enemy face to face
CQMS	Company Quartermaster Sergeant
CSM	Company Sergeant Major
DSO	Distinguished Service Order
FGCM	Field General Court Martial
GHQ	General Headquarters
GOC	General Officer Commanding
HQ	Headquarters
JFS	Jews' Free School
KCB	Knight Commander of the British Empire
MO	Medical Officer
NCO	Non Commissioned Officer
Pte	Private – lowest army rank
RAMC	Royal Army Medical Corps
RQMS	Regimental Quartermaster Sergeant
RSM	Regimental Sergeant Major

RSO	Riding School for Officers
SMLE	Short Magazine Lee Enfield
SS	Steam Ship
TB	Tuberculosis
whizz-bang	Nickname given to a low trajectory, high explosive shell: from the noise it made

Introduction

Dawn, 20 March 2003. Coalition forces, mainly US and British, launched an attack on Saddam Hussein's regime in Iraq. Coalition forces had been built up over a period of several weeks; particular care being taken for the provision of supplies, food and shelter for the troops. Provisions for their welfare and medical care being much to the fore, battle plans were put into effect that would ensure minimal loss of life to Coalition troops and Iraqi civilians.

Dawn, 20 March 1916. A seventeen-year-old British soldier was marched to an embankment and upon the orders of the General Officer Commanding, was shot by his unwilling comrades. In common with them, he had endured seven months of trench warfare, during which time there was little evidence of effective care or welfare, and certainly none of compassion from those put in charge of their fate. His crime was that three weeks after release from medical confinement for wounds and shock, and while in the midst of a bombardment of rifle grenades, he left the line. After eight months in France and several weeks on the line, after receiving wounds and experiencing unremitting deprivations, a frightened boy could take no more and needed respite. For Abraham Bevistein, those few hours of respite were to cost him his life.

Aby's was a life born into turbulent times. A Jewish boy, his life began in a land where Jews were persecuted, where bigotry was condoned and even promoted by those in power, both secular and religious and where a generation later the worst horrors ever perpetrated by the human race were to unfold. Had Aby's family stayed in Warsaw, the chances of him ever reaching a ripe old age were exceedingly slim. As it was, they moved away from the land of his birth, and he was killed at seventeen.

Might he have survived the War had his sentence been commuted? Again, there is a strong chance that he would not have lived past another few weeks, for his battalion and company suffered heavy casualties during the time he was imprisoned and immediately following his execution. And had he beaten the odds and lived through all that, would he have beaten them once again when the East End of London was blitzed night after night in the war that was to follow? Examination of the possibilities holds its own interests, but ultimately it is irrelevant. The fact is that Aby died in a war that claimed the lives of three quarters of a million men and boys of British and Commonwealth armies. Aby died, but first he lived. This is his story.

Chapter 1

Within the Pale

For sufferance is the badge of all our tribe.
William Shakespeare

It was St David's Day in St Petersburg; 1 March (by the old calendar) 1881. Several Cossack guards lay bloody and broken, and Alexander Nikolaevich, the sixty-three-year-old Tsar of all the Russias, went to see the damage that was intended for him. A would-be assassin threw his bomb wide, missing the target. Tsar Alexander II was uninjured; his guards had taken the brunt.

It was then that the student, I. Grinevitskii, threw a second bomb. This time it found its mark and the Tsar was terribly injured. Mortally wounded he died some hours later. The student was not a Jew, and his organization, 'The National Will', had only one Jew within its ranks. But truth ever was a small vessel, easily driven from its course on winds of suspicion and overwhelmed by waves of hatred. The rumour quickened, 'Jews killed the Tsar'. The rumour flourished, not without a little tender care from the authorities, and so, once again, Jews must suffer. Once again, the pogroms began.

Many miles away, in Warsaw, or possibly the Ukraine, little Josef Biberstein was not to know how events would swell out from St Petersburg and eventually carry his future family away from the land of his birth. In 1881 Josef was ten years old, and possibly living in a part of Russia that was once – and would be again – Poland. As far as he was concerned he was a Russian citizen even though he may have harboured feelings of belonging to the Kingdom of Poland. In effect, after decades of losing more and more territory to Russia, Prussia and Austria, Poland ceased to become an independently

3

viable nation in 1795. It was just four years earlier that Catherine II (the Great) had created the infamous 'Pale of Settlement'.

Josef may have wondered whether he was a Russian, or whether he was Polish, but of one thing he was certain; he was a Jew, and within the Pale life was often hard and frequently unfair. Jews were expelled from old Russia and were barred from settling elsewhere but within the Pale, which comprised territories annexed from Poland along the western borders with Prussia and those wrested from the Turks along the shores of the Black Sea. As time went on, other territories were added to the Pale and Jews were permitted to settle as colonizers.

Persecution of the Russian Jews did not begin with the murder of the Tsar. It had been a feature of life to a greater or lesser extent for generations, but events were about to take a definite turn for the worse. It could hardly have been otherwise when the new Tsar was so anti-Semitic. The murdered Tsar had freed the serfs and was on the verge of ratifying the nation's first written constitution. Hopes for it to be brought into law died with the Tsar. His second son and successor, Alexander Alexandrovich, was to be remembered in history as the last true autocrat. He refused to grant the constitution declaring 'full faith in the justice and strength of the autocracy'.

Alexander III came to power and immediately tightened censorship of the press. Thousands of revolutionaries were sent to Siberia and any liberal feelings within the government were swiftly rooted out. To Alexander III autocratic rule was a God-given right and he set about doing all he could to strengthen it. His reign became known as the Age of Counter Reform.

His strong views of autocracy, orthodoxy and nationalism were instilled at an early age. Constantine Petrovich Pobedonostsev, a state official and philosopher who upheld all the old, conservative fundamentals, tutored both Alexander and his older brother Nicholas, who died in 1865. In later years the liberal camp was to denounce him as an enemy of progress, but for now he held sway. Instrumental in the intellectual growth of the new Tsar, he also taught him to be anti-Semitic and to consider his Jewish subjects as 'Christ killers'.

So once again the stage was set for the pendulum to swing towards ill fortune for the Jewish communities of the Russian Empire. The Biberstein family, in common with their neighbours, did their best to weather the storms and to enjoy the occasional sunshine afforded to them by their strong faith and sense of community. From time to time Jews would be attacked simply because they were Jews. Once in a while a house would be vandalized.

The Jews have known such victimization since time immemorial and adversity strengthens community and a desire to help one another. There comes a time though when the bonds of family and community are tried beyond endurance.

It was at this time when Jews, in their thousands, decided enough was enough. There had to be more to life than repression and the fear of loved ones coming to harm at the hands of strangers. Somewhere there had to be a place where people were free to celebrate their faith and to live without hatred blighting their lives. The pogroms of 1881 marked, if not prompted, the beginning of the First Aliyah – a mass movement of Jews, mainly from Eastern Europe, to Palestine. The *Hovevei Zion* (the Lovers of Zion) began the long march home to Eretz-Israel.

Many others turned to the far west, its gateway marked by an emblem of liberty and welcome – a flaming torch held aloft in the hand of a huge statue, which stands on a rock known as Liberty Island. For thousand of Jews, the United States of America became their shining beacon, and in the three decades that followed the assassination of the Tsar Liberator, hundreds of thousands of oppressed Jewish people were to set out on a journey that would alter the face of the world.

For now, the Bibersteins stayed put. Josef grew to manhood and met a young girl – three years his junior – called Riwke. Then in 1894 Alexander III died of nephritis. He was only forty-nine, and barring assassination it was generally believed he would impose his rule for many years to come, but a kidney injured in a railway accident in 1888 led to an early death. His son Nicholas Alexandrovich Romanov was crowned Nicholas III, and Josef Biberstein's twenty-three years now touched the rule of three tsars. Although he was to live to be a comparatively old man, he would see no more tsars and would outlive nearly all the Romanovs.

It is most likely that in the early years of the last Tsar's reign, Josef and Riwke were married. Life was no easier for the Jews nor for the general population of the Empire. Nicholas III made it very clear right from the start that he would guard the fundamentals of autocracy with the same fervour as his father. It would be wrong to suggest that only the Jews were repressed by the regime, for indeed the Polish in general suffered much. Uprisings were put down mercilessly and thousands of Poles died, but the Jewish community always seemed to take the brunt. In the 1790s many Jews joined their fellow Poles in an uprising during the partition period. In response, Russian troops massacred the Jewish civilian population of Warsaw.

Warsaw itself had long been a place of Jewish settlement – as far back as the fourteenth century – and even then Jews were subjected to hostility. In 1483 Jewish inhabitants were expelled from Warsaw, and from 1527 to 1768 they were officially banned from the city. They lived in privately owned settlements called *jurydykas* on the outskirts of the city. Although many Jews were to be found in the city living quiet and unobtrusive lives so as not to stir up the enmity of neighbours, it was not until 1768 that they were openly allowed to live in Warsaw. By 1792 the Jewish population of the city was nearly 7,000.

Ironically the pogroms of 1881 prompted a huge increase in the number of Jews living in Warsaw, for the situation in old Russia was far worse than in the annexed territories. During this period 150,000 Jews moved to Warsaw, many migrating from Lithuania, Belorussia and the Ukraine. If the Bibersteins were not already residents of the city before 1881, there is a little evidence to suggest that they may have been part of this influx from the Ukraine.

Josef and Riwke were probably educated at *hederim*. Ninety per cent of all Jewish children attended a *heder* – small classes often located in the house of a rabbi. Orthodox groups ran the *heder* although the *Hovevei Zion* opened its own *heder* in 1885. To say anything more about the Bibersteins or Riwke's family is not possible unless at some time in the future new evidence comes to light.

By the 1890s the Jewish population of Warsaw was somewhere around a quarter of a million. More than half of those involved in the city's commerce were Jewish. There were doctors, merchants, artists and writers as well as representatives of the whole range of service providers and artisans. We do not know for sure the calling or trade in which Josef was schooled, but there is a high probability that he practised the tailor's trade. Certainly, this was his trade in later times.

As mentioned, Josef and Riwke were married in the early to mid-1890s. On Monday, 18 April 1898 the SS *Duke of Leinster* was berthed in the River Liffey at Dublin when a man suffering from a form of mental illness jumped overboard. William Kay, the ship's chief steward jumped in after him and despite the drowning man's frantic struggles, he held him above water until help came in the form of a small boat. On that same Monday, somewhere in Warsaw, Abraham Biberstein was born. Their firstborn came into an unstable and uncertain part of the world

Two tiny unrelated events, drops that combine with millions of others to form the tide of human history, important only to the individuals concerned and their immediate families. Chief Steward William Kay was cited for a bronze medal by the Royal Humane Society for saving the sick man. When Abraham Biberstein needed saving, not a hand was raised in support, nor was there shown any quality even remotely akin to humanity.

As the nineteenth century drew to a close the Russian people struggled to throw off their bonds and shackles. Riots of peasants, workers and students continued to be crushed by oppression, but with ever less success. One of the ways the government sought to deflect the revolutionary movement was to fan the flames of anti-Semitism. Josef and Riwke now had an infant son to consider, and although not yet a conflagration, the flames spread slowly and inexorably. Then on 5 October 1900 a daughter was born to Josef and Riwke Biberstein. Abraham's sister was named Kate. With the future of two children to consider the Bibersteins probably began to make plans to leave at around this time.

Chapter 2

Exodus

O Captain! my Captain!
Our fearful trip is done,
The ship has weather'd every rack,
The prize we sought is won.
                    Walt Whitman

It would paint an unduly dramatic picture to imply that Josef led his family into exile with the Cossacks hot on their heels. The increasing unrest and the demoralizing prospect of a local pogrom, although undoubtedly factors in Josef's decision to leave Warsaw, only formed part of his reasoning. Poverty, epidemics, the lack of prospects for their children and the hope of a better life in a foreign land must have played on the minds of Josef and Riwke, perhaps even to a greater extent than the fear of violence. Pogroms were a threat dampened by chance – poverty was always present.

It was late in September 1902 when the Bibersteins joined the flow of humanity that departed Central and Eastern Europe. In years past those leaving European shores had tended to be, in the main, travellers and itinerants moving from town to town, country to country, until they settled – often in Britain. But during the last quarter of the nineteenth century and thereafter, because of political, religious and economic pressures, the majority of emigrants were seeking a completely fresh start in the New World.

We do not know what triggered the Bibersteins to leave Warsaw when they did, but it cannot be discounted that they succumbed to the seductive manipulations of locally based shipping agents and their promotional activities. From the 1860s nearly every village had its agent, working as part of a network that covered Central and

Northern Europe. The Baltic trade in cattle, cargo and iron ore had long been carved up between the major shipping magnates of the time, and by 1902 these arrangements extended to human traffic. Between them companies such as Cunard, White Star and Wilson's competed for the custom of the never-ending stream of Russian Jews leaving the Pale. These companies vied for the trade of those who sought an Atlantic crossing leaving from one of the Baltic ports, but the Bibersteins went another way. They chose the overland route, travelling from Warsaw to Rotterdam by rail.

Today the railway journey from Warsaw to Rotterdam could comfortably be achieved within eighteen hours. It was a different matter for the Bibersteins. This is not to say that either the railway network or the rolling stock was incapable of facilitating such a timely trip, for it was perfectly well established all along the route. However, there were procedures to comply with, indignities to endure and sometimes clandestine border crossings to negotiate. Although some people left Russian territory quite legally, one estimate suggests that 90 per cent of Russian emigrants left without being granted official leave, slipping across the frontier. Sometimes officials would turn a blind eye; sometimes bribes would be levied. Many emigrants would have been allowed an official exit, but they had cause not to risk a refusal. One consequence of this mass movement of humanity was the setting up of two opposing but equally vast camps – one to exploit the emigrants and the other to protect them from exploitation.

As September in the year 1902 drew to a close, so the train, bearing amongst its passengers a married couple and their two small children, pulled out of Warsaw. Abraham was four years old and his sister Kate was just over a week short of her second birthday. By now Aby was undoubtedly able to converse in Yiddish at a level commensurate with his age and very likely knew a smattering of the Polish tongue as well.

Once west of Warsaw, the train progressed south-west for some fifty miles before the line branched into two. One line led south towards Cracow, the other towards the north-west roughly following the course of the River Vistula. Crossing into the narrow, southern-most tip of Western Prussia just south of the town of Thorn, the train soon passed into the then German State of Posen. Passing further west and through the towns of Bromberg, Nackel and Schneidenmuhl, the Bibersteins would have then passed into yet another German State – this time Brandenberg. Had they made the same journey sixteen years later, most of the German territories through which they had been travelling would have been part of a much bigger Poland. Some town names would have remained the same, but others would have altered; for example, Schneidenmuhl was renamed as 'Pita' when reclaimed by Poland.

It is also highly likely that the Bibersteins' journey would have been frequently interrupted. Somewhere along the line, the track itself changed from the Russian to the narrower German gauge and there were probably several changes of train involved. Entire networks had been built up around the mass migrations: agents to facilitate the flow and to line their pockets at the same time, customs officials, medical facilities, hostels and control stations. In a chilling premonitory parallel to a more sinister end that was to befall the Jews who stayed in Europe for a generation too long, many migrants passing through the control stations were required to strip off and make their way to large cleansing facilities while their clothing was fumigated. Told by officials that paper money would not survive the fumigation process, the migrants would hold their money in their hands thus providing an opportunity for the unscrupulous to see it and calculate to what extent they could be fleeced.

To cope with the number of migrants, the control stations – some sixty in all – had been set up by the Prussian government in 1891. Here travellers would be medically examined, selected into groups fit to travel on and those rejected, the latter being cared for until they were fit for the onward journey. The aims however, were not particularly altruistic, but rather to supply the German shipping lines with a steady and lucrative stream of customers. Those who had tickets to America with non-German lines were seldom afforded aid. Those claiming to be en route to Britain were closely questioned as to their true destinations and migrants wishing to settle elsewhere in Europe were not helped at all.

To what extent the Bibersteins suffered the deprivations of the journey, or the nature of any aid they may have received, cannot be told. Their circumstances and destination suggest that, within the German Empire at least, assistance was minimal and deprivations high, for evidence suggests that when at last they arrived in England they were close to destitute.

Berlin was probably considered the halfway mark of their travels. Once past Berlin the line went through Spandau and across the State border into Saxony. Crossing the River Elber the journey was probably interrupted at Stendal which was the site of a major railroad intersection. Perhaps there was another change of trains at this point. From here, two separate routes were possible – one heading south for a time before turning once again for the west, and the other following a more northerly route. The northerly one through Hanover was the more direct. Passing through the city of Hanover and then through the final large German town of Osnabrook, the line left the German Empire and entered the Netherlands. Passing through Gelderland and Utrecht both lines eventually reached the sea.

The major ports of Amsterdam and Rotterdam both ran services that catered mainly for the Jewish migrants. The Bibersteins opted for – or were assigned by their agent – the crossing from Rotterdam. Arriving at Rotterdam at the end of September – probably on the 30th – tired and uncomfortable, they now had to make their way to the port and find the berth assigned to the shipping company that would take them to England. It is possible they received some kind of support from the Montefiore Vereiniging, an organization set up in Rotterdam to help the migrants.

Only one major company, the Batavier Line, operated a regular shuttle-like service catering for the migrants out of Rotterdam. Every day, except Mondays, a Batavier Line vessel would discharge its cargo of tired and expectant people onto England's shores. It was a night crossing and the Bibersteins sailed in the 1,136 ton SS *Batavier III*. The little ship had come into service with the line a year before Aby's birth, in 1897, and was eventually sold to Panama in 1939 when it was renamed the *El Sonador*. The ferry-sized vessel, if following the usual timetable and allowing for prevailing conditions at sea, probably arrived at Gravesend at around 6.00 am on Wednesday, 1 October 1902.

There, the little ship picked up a Port of London pilot, then carried on up the Thames to Custom House Quay having first passed underneath the famous Tower Bridge. The Quay being situated on the north bank of the Thames just to the west of the Tower of London, the Bibersteins were thus delivered very close to the East End where the family was to settle for many years. Many long and arduous miles behind them – in excess of 800 as the crow flies, to give

11

some perspective – Josef now had to find somewhere for his family to live.

The Bibersteins arrived in England as refugees, and as immigrants when the word 'immigrant' meant 'Jew'. Spurred by the increasingly intolerable conditions at home they had made their leap into the dark and landed on solid foundations, but the future was far from clear. Whether Josef had set his sights on Britain or had intended it merely as a stopover with America as the final destination, we do not know. We do know that for many who had planned to set up life in the New World, there was disappointment when they discovered they had been sold invalid tickets or they had lost all their money for one reason or another. Whatever their intentions, the Bibersteins stayed. As they gathered their meagre belongings and left the dock behind, they had no home waiting for them. Help was at hand though, in the form of The Poor Jews' Temporary Shelter, just a few streets away.

Originally situated at 19 Church Lane, Whitechapel, the premises had been owned by a Jewish baker, Simha Becker, who allowed it to be used for the purpose of providing temporary shelter for destitute travellers of the faith. Established in 1885 it offered only the most basic and unsanitary of accommodations, originally just a loft where the weary could lay down without even the facility to undress with any decorum. By 1902 the Shelter had relocated to Leman Street. Many thousands of Jewish migrants passed through its doors, the vast majority as a stopgap between their old homes, largely in Eastern Europe, and their new ones either in the New World or in South Africa. Some, like the Bibersteins, were to stay in England.

Thirteen massive registers, containing the names of those who passed through the Shelter, have survived and cover the years from 1896 to 1914. It is from one of these registers that we are afforded the clue that Riwke, Aby and Kate Biberstein stayed at the Shelter for seven days commencing 1 October 1902. Josef, it appears, did not stay. It is probable that he spent his time seeking out more suitable lodgings for his small family and for some form of employment. It is also possible that he remained in Warsaw for a short period, concluding family business, but given the potential dangers of the journey this does not seem at all likely.

After seven days, Riwke and the children left the Shelter for accommodation in Jane Street, parallel and one street along from Anthony Street where the family would grow up and where Riwke would live until her death in 1928. So, their fearful trip was done, and it remained for them to carve out a living from their stark, new haven.

Chapter 3

Haven?

The boy stood on the burning deck,
His mother called him 'lobos'
Because he wouldn't wash his neck
And go to Shul on Shabbos.
                              Traditional: Jewish East End

Jane Street, E1, was in the North Ward of the Parish of St George's-in-the-East. The Bibersteins had arrived in one of the most overcrowded parts of London at the very peak of a housing shortage, caused by the razing of thousands of homes to make way for railway facilities, street improvements, business premises and schools. When homes were demolished, very little if anything at all was done to rehouse the displaced families, and they were left very much to their own devices to find other accommodation, suitable or not. In 1871 there were 8,262 homes in Whitechapel giving shelter to 75,552 people. By 1901 the housing stock had fallen to 5,735, whereas the population had risen to 78,768. This meant that the average number of residents per house rose from an already mighty 9.14 to 13.74. As usual, figures tell us less than first hand accounts, and the following is an extract from a meeting of the London County Council held close to the time of the Bibersteins' arrival at Jane Street.

> In St. George's-in-the-East a man and his wife and their family of eight occupied one small room. This family consisted of five daughters aged twenty, seventeen, eight, four and an infant and three sons aged fifteen, thirteen and twelve.

14

The gentleman who placed this information before the Public Health Committee asked whether or not it was the duty of the local authority to prevent such serious overcrowding.

The housing along Jane Street was terraced, and it was just as well that Josef's family was small, for the narrow houses boasted few rooms. It is likely that Josef rented the upstairs pair of rooms from the family downstairs who in turn rented from another landlord, and maybe even had a lodger sharing one of the downstairs rooms as part of the bargain. Such arrangements were far from uncommon. The street ran south of the Commercial Road, which itself had added to the housing shortage, with terraces and alleys having been carved through to form a highway from the City to the docks.

Two months before the Bibersteins arrived in the East End another young man arrived, answering, if not a call from the wild then at least a desire to experience the wild side of life. He came to walk the streets that would become familiar to Aby. The American author Jack London planned his trip to coincide with the coronation of King Edward VII; and his itinerary, to give him a view from the gutter. He 'carried the banner' with the people who walked the streets at night because they had nowhere to sleep, he rented the basest kind of accommodation and he wore dirty, second-hand clothes. He really meant to see what life was like for the people of the East End, by walking in their shoes, and what he saw almost destroyed his faith in human nature. In the second week of August 1902, after he had been living as a stranded American sailor for just one week, he wrote to a friend immediately after penning some 4,000 words of his proposed work.

> I have just finished. It is one in the morning. I am worn out and exhausted and my nerves are blunted with what I have seen and the suffering it has cost me ... I am made sick by this human hell-hole called the East End.

These words were written by a tired, twenty-five-year-old author who had plumbed the deepest depths of a poor and disenfranchised society, and it must be remembered that not everybody, even in the East End, lived life as he was experiencing. We must allow that he was moved by the lives of the homeless and sickened by the squalor he encountered all about him. He went on to write about his East End sojourn in his book, *The People of the Abyss*, and the opening

15

paragraph of one chapter provides at least one valid view, coming as it does from a man who took the time and made the sacrifices necessary to gain a true insight.

> At one time the nations of Europe confined the undesirable Jews in city ghettos. But today the dominant economic class, by less arbitrary but none the less rigorous methods, has confined the undesirable yet necessary workers into ghettos of remarkable meanness and vastness. East London is such a ghetto, where the rich and the powerful do not dwell, and the traveller cometh not, and where two million workers swarm, procreate, and die.

When Jack had completed his manuscript, he scribbled a note which he appended to the work before posting it to his New York publishers.

> If I were God one hour, I'd blot out all London and its 6,000,000 people, as Sodom and Gomorrah were blotted out, and look upon my work and call it good.

So Josef had brought his little family across hundreds of miles of land and sea to arrive in anything but a haven. Their new home was awash in a sea of slums and dirt and squalor. And yet, a haven may be more than fine buildings and vistas of green parkland. A true haven is a shelter from the storm, and in the East End the Bibersteins found friends, and people who spoke the same language, knew the same towns and gave a familiar feel to a strange land. The Bibersteins came to a community where their Jewish faith put them in the minority and where anti-Semitism was not unheard of, but they were in a very large minority – large enough for any anti-Semite to be very careful about where and how he expressed his bigoted views, and for the Jews to feel very much at home. At least there were no pogroms, and at best they were so surrounded by sounds and sights and people familiar, that until the coming of Zion, it was probably as close to a haven as one could hope to get.

Jack London lived with the down and outs, the homeless and those who had lost their souls to drink. Perhaps he can be forgiven for failing to include the lives of another kind of East End folk, who fought a never-ending battle with the surrounding griminess and dirt, and who worked hard to make the very most of their limited means and to carve out a life for their children. Although he did not write much about them, no doubt he encountered them and he would never forget his short spell as an East Ender. Years later he was to write of his work:

> Of all my books on the long shelf, I love most *People of the Abyss*. No other book of mine took so much of my young heart and tears as that study of the poor.

The Biberstein family cannot have been long in England before the decision was made to anglicize their names. Josef took to using 'Joseph' and Riwke became know by the English version of her name, which was Rebecca. Kate and Abraham's forenames remained the same, but the family name took on a more phonetic spelling. In the Cyrillic alphabet, it was already phonetic. A coat of arms attributed to an East European family called 'Biberstein' includes the representation of a beaver as the main device on the shield, perhaps giving a clue as to the correct pronunciation. Furthermore, the Cyrillic letter that represented the 'v' sound was to Western eyes a 'b'. We can imagine the family's frustration at having their new acquaintances and officials continually mispronouncing their name, sounding a 'b' in the middle instead of a 'v', so it was probably shortly after their arrival that they changed the spelling of their name accordingly. The 'Bibersteins' were now the 'Bevisteins', and so the name remained until the last to bear it passed away.

That they had chosen such a rare rendering of their name has greatly assisted in researching Aby's story. Had they been called 'Bernstein', there would have been no way of telling which of the scores of Aby Bernsteins our Aby was, and his story would have been virtually impossible to tease out.

In one respect, the Bevisteins came to England at a difficult time. Housing was hard to come by and virtually impossible to secure without the payment of key-money, which may explain why Rebecca and the children had to stay at The Poor Jews' Shelter for a week. It is reasonable to assume that Joseph had to work up sufficient funds to make a payment in advance on the Jane Street rooms. On the other hand, they arrived into an established community of people who could empathize with newcomers, for most of them had so recently been in the same situation. However, for those who came in the years immediately following the Russian and Polish pogroms of the early 1880s, understanding from the established Jewish community was not as forthcoming.

In the 1880s, British Jewry was well on the road to assimilation. They kept their faith, but in a quiet and non-ostentatious manner, and were represented in almost all honourable and worthy estates in British life. Industry, commerce, medicine and politics; all benefited from their Jewish acolytes. It was only in the military limb of society that Jews were poorly represented. Religious life was rarely abandoned, but matters secular lost more and more of the trimmings of Jewry. There was almost an air of *Sha sha, the Goyim* – don't upset the Gentiles: Jews wanted to blend in with their neighbours and not draw attention to differences that might make acceptance difficult. This helps to explain how many British Jews felt their security under assault when thousands of East European Jews started flooding into the country, and how it came to be that some prominent Jews were at the forefront of calls to stem the tide of immigration.

For the part of the new immigrants, they did not feel welcome, few spoke their language and the synagogues did not fulfil their requirements. Synagogues had become, much like the majority of Church of England churches, a sacred place to go and worship on the Sabbath. The Jews who flooded in from troubled lands in the East needed their synagogues to be the centre of their communities. Little time passed before they established their own synagogues, numerous and small, and known as *bebrot*, or societies. The singular term was *bebra*, and a *bebra* could be based in an old shop, in part of a dwelling or in an old Christian establishment abandoned by a community moving on. Eventually these many *bebrot* were joined to form the Federation of Synagogues. About twenty years later, when the Bevisteins arrived, feeling at home in a new community was not nearly so hard to achieve.

Joseph quickly found work as a tailor, working long hours in cramped and insalubrious conditions, perhaps in a room below his small home. Rebecca is unlikely to have worked outside the family home, which she would have ruled as keeper of family exchequer. Abraham and Kate would have joined the throng of children to be found playing on the streets, watched over by elderly ladies and old gentlemen who sat on chairs outside their front doors, when the weather allowed. So cramped were conditions indoors that it was common for occupants to make the most of dry days. In the early evenings, men would sit outside smoking, with children at their knees. Papers would be read – some were available in Yiddish – and politics would be discussed, especially anything that involved 'the old homeland'.

Often, conflicts far far away led to consequences right on the doorstep. For example, the year after Joseph settled down with his family, the Russian Empire declined to recognize Japan's interest in Manchuria and Korea. Japan launched an attack on Russian warships at Inchon in Korea, and at Port Arthur in China, and invaded the disputed territories in 1904.

'Interesting,' an Englishman may have thought. 'But so far away, it will not affect me.'

'Ah but think again,' may well have been the rejoinder from a more politically aware Jew from the East End. 'Always there are consequences.'

There were very few major events which did not affect the Jew. Either he would be made a scapegoat, moved on because someone else wanted his home or enrolled against his will to achieve an objective not to his benefit. In the case of the Russo-Japanese War, the Tsar soon found that his losses were immense, and began to conscript men into the armed forces of Imperial Russia. One consequence of this was that thousands of young Jewish men began to arrive in London, not willing to be conscripted for service in Siberia. The East End Jews responded with donations for food and shelter, and feeding centres were set up in the synagogues. Even free steam baths were set up, and all this was achieved in just a few days.

Always there are consequences. The Russo-Japanese War also brought the world a step closer to a war, the scale and scope of which even the most politically aware could not begin to imagine.

Meanwhile, little Aby settled into the East End *Yiddishkeit* – the Yiddish way of life. He may have started to pick up the odd English phrase or two from his early encounters with English children, but it is probably the case that he began no formal training in his new tongue until he started school in the Autumn term of 1904, when he was six year old. Neither his father nor his mother spoke any English, so it was strictly 'Yiddish' at home.

Aby may well have been attending a *heder*, much as his father had likely done in Poland, for many of these had been set up to cater for the religious education of Jewish boys and girls, and attendance usually began at a very young age. But on 22 August 1904, Aby was enrolled into one of the many large schools, which towered above the local houses like dark battleships. Although there is some evidence that Aby had previously attended the Infants section of the school, there is no record of him in the infants' register.

Aby became a scholar at Lower Chapman Street School. By now the Bevisteins had moved to 8 Fenton Street, E1 – parallel with and two streets to the west of Jane Street. It ran south from the Commercial Road and ran down to form a T-junction with Lower Fenton Street. Aby's route to school took him in this direction, where he would then have turned left into Lower Fenton Street, right into Agar Place – a short alley – and so across Lower Chapman Street and into school. From front door to schoolyard, all within about five minutes.

At the time of writing, Fenton Street, like Jane Street and Anthony Street are no more than cobbled stubs of roads junctioning with the Commercial Road, and Lower Fenton Street has disappeared altogether. Lower Chapman Street remains, but since the 1930s has been known as Bigland Street. Aby's old school though, is still there after all these years, looking much as it did then, but now afloat in a sea of maisonettes. It escaped the blitz, which devastated all but one of the places where the Bevisteins lived. It is still used as a school, and was in fact the school attended by Aby's nieces in the 1930s – Kate's children whom Aby was never to meet.

It was – and still is – an impressively large building, and typical of its breed, a giant three-decker. More than 1,000 boys crammed into its classes when Aby was a scholar, almost half of them Jewish. A week after he started school, a headcount showed a total of 712 Jewish children: 227 boys, 197 girls and 288 infants. Although it was not a Jewish school, it would often close on the occasion of Jewish holidays. An older boy at the school, whom Aby would soon get to know, was Alec Kutchinsky who lived at 48 Anthony Street, which ran south from the Commercial Road, flanked by Jane Street and Fenton Street.

In his fourth week at school, a headcount of an entirely different kind took place, when the London County Council nurse attended 'to inspect the heads of the boys' for head-lice. This practice continued at least until the 1960s, for the author can clearly remember standing in line to benefit from the ministration of the 'nit-nurse' when in junior school.

Many boys of Aby's age and situation attended the Jews' Free School, commonly known by its initials, which was then located in

Middlesex Street – better known as Pettycoat Lane – but it was quite a trek for a small lad and would have added considerably to the length of his school day. It made sense to send him to a school just a few minutes walk down the road, though his neighbour from two doors up – closer to the Commercial Road on the west side of Fenton Street – did make the journey. Nick Rosansky lived at number 4, and coincidentally was born on the same day as Aby. It is inconceivable that the two boys did not know each other, and highly probable that they were friends, playing games together with other children in their street-based 'playgrounds'. Curiously, it appears Nick left the JFS for a short period and went to Lower Chapman Street School, but after only a week, he returned to the JFS.

Aby's headmaster was John James McCubbin, who had been promoted to the post from Betts Street School in August 1901. During Aby's second term at Lower Chapman Street he held an examination, and his report highlights some of the problems of the day.

> The lower division of Standard 2 contains a weak section, due to the number of foreigners and to the class containing some Jew boys below the average of intelligence.
> The teacher is working well in his endeavours to bring the class to the required standard.

It was around this time that Mr Pinkus Harris joined the school staff as an assistant teacher on supply. A week later, on Monday, 17 July 1905, the school closed so that the children could go on a day-trip organized by 'Pearson's Fresh Air Fund'. The Fund – which is still viable today – was started in 1892 by the founder of the *Daily Express*, Sir Arthur Pearson, and it was founded so that children from the slums could get away from the grime and sooty air, and just for a day, enjoy the countryside 'for just ninepence a head, to include railway fares and a plentiful supply of good food'. A song penned to help raise funds became well known, and contained the following verse.

> Give me the price of a bit of ribbon,
> Only the cost of a good cigar;
> And we'll take them away for a long happy day
> Out in the fields where the daisies are.

Trips were commonly to locations such as Epping Forest, and children whose only contact with animals was the butcher's dog and mangy old cats, were enthralled to see a cow or a flock of sheep. By 1911, two million children had benefited from the Fund, which was well supported. For many children, it was their only chance to see beyond their cramped and smoky horizons.

Mr Harris was already settling in and was noted as 'working well'. He was soon to be taken on as a permanent member of staff, and would in fact be Aby's teacher. Could it be that when Aby needed to choose an English-sounding name, 'Harris' sprang to mind because it was the name of his old teacher?

Aby went to school at a time when the 'Standards' system had been in place for many years. The eldest children at the top of the school were in Class 1 and they studied to achieve Standards 7 and 8. In 1905 they were expected to recite from *Haratius*. The youngest children were in Class 9, and their objective was to satisfy the requirements of Standard 1, and to be able to recite from *Running After the Rainbow*. The lower standards, that is 1 and 2, were taught to read by the Sonnenschien method.

It was some time during Aby's first year at school that the Bevisteins moved home again, and if his walk to school had been short, now it was but a few steps. Their new home was at 39 Lower Chapman Street, which was right on the corner with Anthony Street. Aby was beginning his second year at Lower Chapman Street School and Kate now joined him. Many other children however, were absent from the first day of the new school year, due to hop picking. On 9 October 1905, half the boys were absent. It was the Day of Atonement and the school logbook tells us that all the Jewish boys were absent, so we can extrapolate that at this time half the boys were Jewish. Also absent were the Jewish masters, Mssrs Harris, Hizer, Rosenberg A., Rosenberg J. and Solomons. The following week, the school was closed on the occasion of King Edward VII opening Aldwych and Kingsway.

Being so close to the school, it is likely Aby and Kate used to go home at midday for lunch, but commencing Monday, 4 December 1905, another option was opened to them.

Dinners for Jewish children commenced today and will be given on Mon. Tues. Wed & Thurs at Berners Street School.

22

To overcome the difficulty of providing the Jewish children with kosher meals, and the Christian children with fare they were more used to, mealtimes were staggered, and the following day the school began serving the Christian children breakfast 'on Tues. Wed. Thurs & Fri'.

Aby was seven years old at this time, and when not studying under the tutelage of Mr Pinkus Harris, the remainder of his day was probably split between helping Rebecca with household chores and running errands for her, more study at the *heder* and playing with his friends. For *heder*, it would have been just a short walk for him to attend the Christian Street *Talmud Torah* where he would have received instruction in Hebrew and religious practices. It must have seemed a great joke to the lads that they received their religious instruction in a street named as it was. Arriving home from school, he would have had time to eat tea, put on his *tsitit-confus* (a four cornered undervest with a fringe, or *tsitse* at each corner) and then make the ten minute walk west along the Commercial Road with the trams running up and down the lines, which were embedded along the centre of the road. We can perhaps imagine Rebecca scrubbing his knees before sending him off with his *tsitit-confus* tucked in. The garment was worn as a reminder that God is present in all corners of the earth. The extremely pious would wear theirs untucked so that the *tsitses* were visible hanging over the trousers and below the jacket (if worn), but it was common in Aby's day for boys living in close proximity to Christian neighbours to tuck them in. It was also common for Jewish boys and men to refrain from the wearing of a skullcap, and there is photographic evidence to suggest that Aby was no different from the majority in this respect.

If Aby did attend the *Talmud Torah* in Christian Street, it is likely his walk home may have been eventful on occasion. Christian Street was on the edge of what was considered the Jewish stronghold, and sometimes rough, loutish Christian boys would wait for the class to turn out so they could torment the Jewish boys, throwing stones and calling them 'Yids'.

When he had completed his secular and religious studies for the day, and there were no more domestic chores or errands, how did Aby spend his time? Here we may only assume that Aby was typical of the boys of his age, and speak in terms of what boys generally found to do for fun. Toys were a rarity, but why would a boy need toys anyway when he had the cobbled streets as his playground?

Full use was made of kerbs for games of marbles, just as paving stones were. Leap-frog was played, either over other boys' backs or over street furniture. Two streets up from Jane Street, west along the Commercial Road is Rampart Street. In Aby's day it was called Little Turner Street, but today, apart from the name, it is much the same as it would have been in Aby's day. Sly Street runs off it; both are still cobbled and at the junction of the two is an old, iron, cannon-shaped bollard. It is dated, so we know it was there when Aby was a boy, and it is easy to imagine him leap-frogging over it with a procession of other small boys.

Other games known to him would have been hopscotch, not then thought of as a girls' game. Numbered squares were chalked on the pavement and the players had to hop from one square to another in a certain order, sometimes stooping to pick up strategically placed stones. As spirits rose, so hopscotch may have developed into a robust game of Hop and Barge, which involved the bargers shoulder-charging the hoppers to put them off balance. Then there was 'Hi Jimmy Knacker', a rough game for two teams of four or more boys. One boy of the first team stood with his back up against a wall. The second boy would make a back by stooping and placing his head against the first boy's stomach. Each subsequent team member would make a back by placing his head between the legs of the boy in front and gripping his thighs. It was then the aim of the second team to cause this living structure to collapse, by leaping onto the long, multiple-back while shouting, 'Hi Jimmy Knacker, one, two, three.'

Then of course, there were games with cigarette cards. Flicking, flipping, stacking, knocking down; just for fun or for 'keepsies'; rules fluid and changing. Football played with no goals, tennis played with no nets and pieces of wood for rackets: the inventiveness of children and their determination to extract as much fun from their stark environs was never-ending. At the end of the day, Aby went home happy and completely oblivious to the fact that the world considered him one of the poor. With such fun to be had, and parents who loved you, how could a small boy feel anything but privileged?

Rebecca did the best she could with soap, water and a flannel, and so Aby went to bed – one full day ending, another day in the wings. Baths were a weekly event, and although water supplies in the area had improved since a 1903 Act of Parliament established the Public Water Authority, they did not stretch to household bathrooms. When he was little, Aby may have been bathed in the sink, but after that it would have been a weekly visit to the public baths.

Sometimes there was more to school than just work. We have already seen that there was the occasional excursion, and although not a Jewish school, Lower Chapman Street children took part in some of the contests organized by the Jewish Athletic League. In June of 1906, the 1st and 2nd eleven of Aby's school did very well in the football contest and won the Howard Challenge Cup. The winning teams, who had been successful in all their matches, were photographed on the morning of 5 June. A fortnight later, fifty lucky boys were taken on a trip to London Zoo 'on the invitation and expense of Mrs Neahams, one of the managers'.

It was to the school's great shame that six months after winning their sporting trophy a less than sporting specimen of humanity tarnished their reputation. The school log entry for 13 December 1906 records the loss.

> The Howard Challenge Cup won by the football teams in the Jewish League was stolen during the night of Wednesday 12th inst or early morning of Thursday.
>
> No clue has as yet been found to lead to the recovery of the cup or the arrest of the thief.

The are no subsequent entries concerning the Cup, or the thief, so we may assume that both remained undisclosed.

The is no record as to when the Bevistein family moved again, although this may be evident on the publication of future census returns, but it was around about now that they left 39 Lower Chapman Street and moved a few hundred yards north from the junction, to take up residence in the upstairs of 48 Anthony Street. The house had three floors and a basement, with the Bevisteins moving into the two rooms on the first floor and the single attic room. It is possible that the accommodation was made available when the Spieler family moved out. Samuel, a tailor's presser from Austria, his Russian wife Mary and their locally born son Nathan had lived there before. Downstairs, the basement and ground floor, was the home of the Kutchinsky family. The two families shared the tiny back garden with its very large tree and outside toilet.

Michael, a tailor, and Rose Kutchinsky had emigrated from Poland with their daughter Esther. They arrived in England in the early 1880s, just as the influx from Eastern Europe began following the troubles sparked by the assassination of Tsar Alexander II. In 1884 Rose gave birth to a son, Solig. There followed three more sons, Aaron, Isaac and Alec (spelt 'Alick' in some records and 'Aleck' in others), and then another daughter, Rachel. Michael Kutchinsky and Joseph Bevistein may have worked together. Michael may even have been Joseph's boss, the accommodation being tied to the job – we do not know. What is known, however, is that the families became the closest and dearest of friends.

The Kutchinsky children were all older than Aby and Kate, but the Bevisteins and Alec were students at Lower Chapman Street School at the same time for a number of years. Alec left school in March 1908 about a year after his bar mitzvah at which it is reasonable to assume that Aby and the rest of the Bevisteins were guests.

An important event in the life of every Jewish boy, it marked the point when, in religious terms, a boy became a man. To be more precise, he became a man of the word, which is the literal translation of the term bar mitzvah. As Aby watched Alec reading from the Torah, he may have reflected on his own bar mitzvah – but to a young boy, those few years would have felt further away than the distant horizon. When you are eight, four years is half-a-life away; plenty of time to play and learn and grow.

Aby's thirteenth birthday was on 18 April 1911, and his bar mitzvah would have been held some time around this date. He had already left school. As with much of Aby's story, we have the smallest of clues with which to work, but there is an indication that the Bevisteins attended the Great Garden Street Synagogue. Standing, as the name suggests, in Great Garden Street (now called Greatorix Street) just to the north of the Whitechapel Road, it was the centre of administration for the Federated Synagogues. Although no longer a synagogue, the building still stands today.

In the weeks leading up to the big day, Aby would have had time to prepare for his bar mitzvah, learning his *Parsha* (an extract from the Bible) or *Sefer Torah*, and being taught the mysteries of the *tallus* and *teffilin*. The *tallus* was a prayer shawl, and the *teffilin* were phylacteries comprising two small boxes, or *beitim*, one with a long strap and the other with a shorter, looped one. The boxes contained four portions of the *Torah*, two from the Book of Exodus and two from the Book of Deuteronomy. The symbolism in their use was designed to remind the bar mitzvah that he was bound, both in mind and heart to God.

The mysteries of the *teffilin* were taught, and Aby learnt to take off his jacket and bare his left arm. If the weather was cold, it was perfectly acceptable to slide one's left arm out of the jacket, the empty sleeve dangling, and to proceed from there. Next, the *tallus* was put on, and then the box with the long strap was held against the top of the biceps of the left arm and the strap wound round to keep it in place – firmly but not too tight. The box was supposed to be at heart-level when the arm was lowered. The strap was wound round the upper arm three times to form the shape of the Hebrew letter *Sh'in*. Then it was wound a further seven times round the lower arm, and then round the palm of the hand three times to form the letter *Daled*. The second box was then offered up to the forehead with the left hand and the looped strap pulled over the head. The strap was then tightened, the knot of the strap at the nape of the neck. The ends of the strap were then brought over the shoulder and wrapped three times round the middle finger to form the letter *Yod*. The three letters together formed the Hebrew word *Shaddai*, which is one of God's names, and the position of the two boxes symbolized the coming together of head and heart when in prayer.

The big day arrived, and Aby would have walked along the Commercial Road with Joseph, dressed in their best clothes. It is highly likely that Aby's suit was made for him by his father. Perhaps he felt a little self-conscious in his wing-collar and white bow tie. He wore a jacket with wide pin stripes over a waistcoat, and trousers of a plain, darker material tucked into highly polished black boots. Rebecca and Kate probably stayed behind preparing for the special meal in honour of the event. They would get to *Shul* – the synagogue – in time to see Aby become bar mitzvah.

The service would have begun as usual with the *Chazen* or Cantor taking his place on the platform, known as the *Bima*. We can imagine Aby casting his eye, every now and again, towards the ladies' gallery, until he was sure that Rebecca and Kate had arrived, and then he could turn his attention back to his forthcoming contribution to his day.

The *Sefer Torah* is now carried out from the Holy Ark. Readings begin and blessings for portions of the law are said, each man wearing his *tallus*. Then Aby is called, and he climbs up to the *Bima* standing between the *Chazen* and the *Shammas*, or Sexton. Aby takes a deep breath, and sings the blessings that precede the portion of the law that he is to read. Long studied and often practised, Aby's eyes follow the silver pointer held by the *Chazen* and reads the Hebrew words. He reads alone, but he knows he is far from alone, every member of the congregation willing him to do well, many pairs of lips forming the shape of the words he is speaking. And then his part is played, and a weight lifts from his shoulders. The women in the gallery share in Rebecca's pride; the men remember, with a tug of nostalgia, the time when they became bar mitzvah.

The reading and the singing over, Aby can relax and listen as the Rabbi gives his sermon, or *drusha*. Now Kate is probably as excited as Rebecca is proud, for another tradition is approaching. At the appropriate time, after the Rabbi presents Aby with a copy of the *Singer's Prayer Book*, Kate joins with others in the gallery, and rains down sweets on her brother. The service ends, Aby and his friends pick up the sweets – a rare old scramble and a reminder that the new man is still a boy, at least for a few years yet. But he is now bar mitzvah, and in future services, he will take his place with the other men.

And so the new bar mitzvah embarked on another stage of life, school behind him and a life of hard work ahead. Although there was trouble in the Balkans, this was nothing new, and nobody predicted that the Great War – which even at this time was being spoken of in some circles – was to be quite so great and all encompassing as it was to become.

What was there to do for a young, Jewish working boy in the East End? It is likely that work took up much of his time, and that he followed in his father's footsteps and learnt the tailor's trade. Again, we do not know this for sure, and can only rely on the uncertain law of probability. There were few opportunities for a boy of basic education and poor background, but success could be won by hard work. There was also the advantage of his parentage.

> The zeal of Jewish parents for their children's advancement is very noticeable. For this end they will make every sacrifice.

It was a common worry to the parents of Jewish youths that their offspring would go astray, succumbing to the temptations of the music halls, picture palaces or other less suitable means of entertainment. Like youth the world over, Jewish youth had the capacity to scandalize the older generation. Cutting *Shul* in favour of a stroll down the Whitechapel Road was bad enough, but then to duck into establishments thought taboo – what was the world coming to?

> At a most critical stage in a boy's life, when the undeveloped character is most susceptible to external influences, good or bad, he was left to shift for himself ... His leisure hours spent in aimless loafing about the streets, or occasional visits to low places of entertainment, proper facilities for passing his spare time in a healthy and rational manner, being virtually non-existent.

Enter the Jewish Lads' Brigade and the Brady Street Club for Working Lads, both well established by the time Aby was embarking upon those difficult years.

The Jewish Lads' Brigade was based on military groundings, much as was the Church Lads' Brigade. Members wore uniform and virtues such as physical fitness, punctuality and personal cleanliness were promoted. Summer camps were organized along the lines of military exercises and newsletters took the style of communiqués.

For those young men who had a less militaristic outlook, various clubs sprang up to cater for their needs and safeguard their virtue. Established in 1896, the Brady Street Club was one of the first, and certainly the best known. Its goal was to:

> establish a social and recreational centre for working lads fresh from school, to improve their stunted physique, raise their general tone and bearing, inculcate into them habits of manliness, straightforwardness and self respect.

The Brady Street Club was not initiated as a club primarily for Jewish youth, but it soon came to be so. Although membership was open to all working lads, its membership was almost exclusively Jewish. It offered a range of activities, including a variety of sports, indoor games, summer rambles and camps. It also had a library and catered for those interested in drama. Although membership was limited by the available accommodation, many other similar clubs opened in the wake of the Brady Street Club, including the Stepney Jewish Lads'

29

Club and the Victoria Boys' Club. By the time Aby was eleven years old, these had been drawn under the umbrella of the newly established Association for Jewish Youth.

Aby turned sixteen in April 1914. He was past the age when loving parents and a warm place to sleep enfold one from the harsh realities of the world. His prospects, at best, were to work hard at his trade with a hope that, one day, he may grow successful enough to employ staff and run a modest company. He was at the age when boyish hopes of great achievement and adventure have not been wiped out by the daily grind, and still hover on the misty horizon; when a young man hooks his dreams on impossible heights. For Aby and thousands of other young men like him, the horizon was but three months away.

Chapter 4

A Family Affair

The hand that signed the treaty bred a fever,
And famine grew, and locusts came;
Great is the hand that holds dominion over
Man by a scribbled name.

Dylan Thomas

The British Army, by order of courts martial, knowingly shot thirty-two of their own soldiers who were under the age of twenty-one at the time of execution. Several were only nineteen; some were as young as seventeen. Aby was a month short of his eighteenth birthday when he was killed, but he had lied about his age, like many others. The Army showed him as twenty-one on his death certificate, which puts him even above the age he would have attained under the false details given, which was nineteen. The fact remains that many young men were put to death for military offences.

Contrast this with the Austro-Hungarian Empire, whose courts sentenced a young man called Gavilo Princip to twenty years imprisonment for an offence, albeit not a military one, that carried the death penalty. Their law did not allow a person to be executed if he or she was under the age of twenty when they committed the offence. Princip may have been twenty – his date of birth was not certain. He was either twenty, or perhaps he was just under at nineteen years and eleven months. He was given the benefit of the doubt and sentenced on the premise that he was born in July 1894. His crime; on 28 June 1914 he assassinated Archduke Franz Ferdinand, heir to the Austro-Hungarian throne, and the Archduke's wife.

Two opposing empires, one portrayed as upright and decent, the other militaristic, expansive and plainly the aggressor. And yet by the laws of the former a seventeen-year-old boy could be put to death for being frightened beyond his endurance, while in the latter a nineteen-year-old was spared execution for the offence of killing the heir to the throne and the future empress.

But we are not comparing like with like. Military law, by virtue of its intention (which is to maintain discipline and ultimately to enable armies to be successful in battle) must bear elements that are not reflected in civil law. There comes a stage however, when intention and process are outweighed by levels of culpability, and in the examples shown above, there can hardly be any comparison.

We move back to those days following the death of Franz Ferdinand. He and his wife are dead. Aby is still alive and moving along in the tide of events. How could the killing of a monarch-to-be in a far off country lead to Aby (and hundreds of thousands of others like him) signing up for the hardships of war? We will examine this, and look briefly at how Franz Ferdinand's assassination may be likened to the flicking away of a supporting jack at the base of a wobbly house of cards. Why did his killing bring the world toppling down? We will also see how the War affected the Jewish community of which Aby was part, and we will examine Aby's standpoint as a Jew of immigrant status who was neither compelled nor even eligible to take the King's shilling.

Many have called the Great War a 'family affair'. Through Queen Victoria, several European Heads of State were related. Their last great gathering being at the funeral of Edward VII, when no less than nine kings were in attendance. George V, Kaiser Wilhelm II and Tsar Nicholas Romanov were all cousins. King Edward's daughter Maud was Queen of Norway, and his two nieces were to become Queens of Spain (Ena) and Romania (Marie). Despite all these filial connections, they were to have little influence on events, which were chiefly governed by a tangled knot or treaties and alliances, born for the most part in the wake of the unification of previously independent German States.

The assassination of the Archduke and his wife, the Duchess Sophia, sparked off what has since been called the July Crisis. The Austro-Hungarian Empire had long had designs on parts of Serbia, and indeed already held territory to which Serbia had a claim. Now it seemed the Empire had been supplied with a legitimate reason for invading Serbia. Were the Archduke's assassins not Serbian? Had they not been put up to their dastardly deed by the Serbian government? The latter, at least, has never been proved, but Austro-Hungary grasped at the opportunity.

In a move leading the British Foreign Secretary, Lord Grey, to comment that he had 'never before seen one State address to another independent State a document of so formidable a character', Austro-Hungary issued an ultimatum to Serbia, to the effect that it demanded the assassins be brought to justice. Presuming the power and authority to demand anything of another State was tantamount to stripping it of its own sovereignty. Austro-Hungary was banking on the premise that Serbia would be so offended by the lack of diplomacy in the communication, that she would reject the demand out of hand, thereby giving the larger power a pretext for launching a punitive war. The war would be sharp and swift, for Serbia was but a weak power. But just on the off chance that Serbia tried to enlist the help of Russia, Austro-Hungary first secured a promise of help, in that event, from Germany.

Serbia did not in fact reject the ultimatum out of hand, but merely prevaricated over some minor clauses. Not wishing to miss a narrow window of opportunity, Austro-Hungary used this as an excuse for military intervention, and declared war on Serbia on 28 July 1914. Now the house of cards was nudged beyond saving.

Austro-Hungary had misjudged Russia's reaction to the crisis believing she would merely launch a tirade of words, carefully rounded off by the application of diplomacy, protesting about the molestation of her Slavic brethren. In the event, she began to mobilize her armies. The Bear, swiftly roused was slow to stir, and it was estimated that it would take six weeks for the Russian Army to reach battle readiness. Germany saw Russian mobilization as an act of war, and following a brief flurry of communiqués between Tsar Nicholas and Kaiser Wilhelm, who were cousins, Germany declared war on Russia on 1 August.

Cue France, who had a treaty with Russia. France, who had long hoped to regain lands lost to the Germans in the Franco-Prussian War of 1871, now saw an opportunity to get them back. And conveniently enough, the treaty allowed her to come to Russia's aid, which she did by declaring war on Germany on 3 August 1914.

Although sandwiched between two enemies, the Russians to the east and France to the west, the odds were still stacked in favour of the German and Austro-Hungarian alliance. Of course, Britain had a treaty with France, but with nothing for the Lion to gain, Germany banked on Britain minding its own business and turning an imperial head towards more profitable concerns. As for the seventy-five-year-old Treaty of London in which Britain guaranteed to maintain Belgium – it was just a rather faded scrap of paper.

But the Lion, like the Bear, was stirred. Britain may have had trouble convincing her people that troubles concerning France and far-flung empires were of sufficient concern for them to commit to war, but then Germany went too far. In her rush to secure success on her west, by thrashing France before Russia could mobilize on the east, Germany tore across Belgium after being refused passage. Belgium put up a surprisingly fierce fight for one of the smaller powers. Germany was fierce in her onslaught, and a number of atrocities against the Belgian civilian population ensued, one particularly large in scale.

Stirred up by emotive reports circulated in the media, the British public were incensed and swarmed into the streets crying for war. Britain invoked the terms of the 1839 treaty and declared war on Germany on 4 August 1914.

In the East End of London, the Jewish population was coming to terms with an 'about face' in their traditional views on European politics. Russia was the traditional enemy, her hands red with Jewish blood after pogroms and atrocities spanning generations. The *Jewish Chronicle* had printed editorials suggesting that Britain could never be allied to such an evil empire, and that the British had nothing against the Germans. This all changed in that frantic run down to war. If established Anglo-Jewry was united in one secular area above all others, it was to show their Britishness and loyalty to the country in which they now lived. It would hardly do to speak out against Russia, now an important ally, in favour of Germany who was even now trampling over Belgium to reach France. Perhaps sensing the mood of the people, the *Chronicle* put loyalty before the experiences of history, and demanded that British Jews should do their duty for King and Country. Three days after Britain's declaration of war on Germany, the *Jewish Chronicle* expressed its newfound view with patriotic fervour. Dismissing Russia's continued persecution of the Jews as a misunderstanding, the self-styled voice of the Jewish people reaffirmed Jewish loyalty to the Crown.

England has been all she could be to the Jews; the Jews will be all they can to England.

Stirring stuff for young men keen for adventure, swiftly to be followed up by the publication of Lord Kitchener's famous poster: 'Your King and Country Need You. A CALL TO ARMS'. With Kitchener staring along his pointed finger, aiming it like a rifle at anyone who looked, and the words of the *Jewish Chronicle* fresh in his mind, Aby like many others of his age, was drawn to be part of something exciting and righteous, and so much bigger than the East End life that fate seemed to have set for him. But would he answer the call? Kitchener's call was for volunteers. No man or lad was forced to take the shilling at this time. Furthermore, when two years into the War conscription was put into effect, lads like Aby were exempt as their immigrant status meant they were not British subjects.

Prior to the introduction of conscription in 1916, an estimated 10,000 Jews had volunteered for service, with a little over 10 per cent of that number being commissioned as officers. The majority of these were indigenous or naturalized Jews. Recruiting offices were instructed that a volunteer would be considered British if he was born in Britain, even if his family origin lay in enemy territory; but immigrant, non-naturalized Jews could not be forced to join up. There were between 25,000 and 30,000 Jews of 'fighting' age who would not volunteer. Some were the children of men who had fled Russia to avoid the draft at the time of the Russo-Japanese War. Some had an intense hatred of anything remotely military, and having suffered for so long could not reconcile the lessons of history with the practicalities of fighting on the same side as Russia. Yet others would not infringe the precepts of their religion, as they surely would have to, if they signed up to serve as a soldier.

There were other reasons why immigrant Jews did not wish to join up. In some cases, it was made quite clear that anti-Semitism was alive and well, and that the Army had quite enough Jewish soldiers already. 'Lord Kitchener does not want any more Jews in the Army' and 'We are not enlisting Jews' were examples quoted by the *Jewish Chronicle* of anti-Semitism displayed at recruiting offices as late as 1915. Many East End lads had spent their entire lives within their small, Yiddish-speaking community, never leaving except maybe to pick hops or to go on a day-trip arranged by their schools. The simple prospect of leaving their homes, and their community, which represented a security of sorts, into an army that did not cater for their religious needs and did not really want them anyway, must have been the deciding factor for many otherwise eligible young men.

However, Aby was not among them. By November 1914, 4,000 Jews had joined the colours, and Abraham Bevistein was one of them.

Chapter 5

To the Colours!

Up, lad, up, 'tis late for lying:
Hear the drums of morning play;
Hark, the empty highways crying
'Who'll beyond the hills away?'
A.E. Houseman

Aby did not waste much time in answering Lord Kitchener's call. He took the King's shilling in September 1914 and was therefore in the vanguard of the hundreds of thousands of men and boys who signed up with the New Army. He was sixteen-and-a-half years old, and therefore under the official joining age of nineteen, but the age limit was a little piece of officialdom that put off very few. A mere rule was not going to deter boys who were stirred up with the fervour of the day, and were excited by the prospect of earning the respect of their communities by 'going for a soldier'. It was also a rule made for the breaking by recruiting officers who signed on boys as young as thirteen as we shall see later when we look at the story of Joseph Rosenbloom, a young contemporary of Aby's who was a scholar at the Jews' Free School.

Before signing up, Aby had to present himself for a medical, held at the recruiting office. It was not a particularly detailed examination, and being free of TB, which was still endemic among the working classes at the time, and having good eyesight, a full set of teeth and no obvious defects in his cardio-vascular system, he was passed as fit for service. We can hardly be surprised that a sixteen-and-a-half-year-old lad was passed as eighteen or nineteen, considering boys of thirteen, fourteen and fifteen were also passed.

Following this he would have been attested and then given instructions. Some recruits were told to go straight from the recruiting office to the training depot, but more often than not they would return home to wait for further instructions.

George Coppard, another sixteen-year-old, joined a battalion that would form part of the same division as Aby – the 12th – a few days before, and he documented an experience in his book, *With a Machine Gun to Cambrai*, that must have been widespread, not to say common. (George Coppard was to have a fleeting but poignant connection with Aby, as we will see later.)

> I presented myself to the recruiting sergeant at Mitcham Road Barracks, Croydon. There was a steady stream of men, mostly working types, queuing to enlist. The sergeant asked me my age, and when told, replied, 'Clear off son. Come back tomorrow and see if you're nineteen, eh?' So I turned up again the next day and gave my age as nineteen. I attested in a batch of a dozen others and, holding up my right hand, swore to fight for King and Country. The sergeant winked as he gave me the King's shilling, plus one shilling and ninepence ration money for that day.

So, Aby was far from unique in giving a false age. It has been estimated that some 15 per cent of New Army men enlisted under age. With such a large number under arms, it is only logical to assume that without them our armies would not have been able to withstand the enemy or to emerge from the War victorious. Perhaps the blind eye that was often turned by recruiting sergeants was born of blind eyes all the way up the line, even as far up as the War Office. That they were unaware of large numbers of under-age soldiers is beyond belief. In France, there was even a camp for them, of which James Owen Hannay (G.A. Birmingham) speaks in his book, *With a Padre in France*.

> Their existence in camp was a standing menace to discipline. Officially they were men to be trained, fed, lodged and if necessary punished according to the scheme designed for and in the main suitable to men. In reality they were boys, growing boys, some of them not sixteen years of age, and a few – the thing seems almost incredible – not fifteen. How the recruiting authorities at home ever managed to send a child of less than

fifteen out to France as a fighting man remains a mystery. But they did.

As a boy from the Jewish community, it was unremarkable that Aby enlisted under an assumed name. He signed up as Abraham Harris and was given the number 1799. Why did he feel the need to become Harris for the duration? Based on comments by Sylvia Pankhurst, who took up Aby's case as we shall discover later, some authors give the following, and I believe not entirely thorough, explanation.

It was apparently considered, in some Jewish circles, dishonourable for one's son to become a soldier. Many saw militarism or anything related to it as synonymous with repression. This, it is reasoned, is why Aby signed up as Harris. Of course there may be some truth in this and indeed it may have been a factor in Aby's decision, but there are two other reasons to consider. The name 'Bevistein' is very rare, to the extent that a worldwide search reveals only one, not concerning Aby, who was a German author. However, 'Biberstein' is far more common, and several families with this name can be traced to German held territories. It is at least likely then, that Aby did not wish to go to war with a name that suggested he might have links with the other side.

There is a far more fundamental possibility to consider. There is no trace of Aby or any of his immediate family becoming naturalized citizens of Britain, so Aby was in actual fact a Russian subject living in England. As such he was ineligible for military service at the time he joined. It was not until May 1916 – two months after Aby's death and four after the introduction of conscription – that the War Office announced that it would allow friendly aliens to volunteer for the British Army.

Yet another reason may have been the wish to avoid any anti-Semitism. In Aby's case this is unlikely. Evidence strongly suggests he kept his faith, at least to the extent that he would have been recognized as a Jew despite his change of surname. Also, he joined the Middlesex Regiment. The Duke of Cambridge's Own, to give its other name, had such a high proportion of Jews serving within its ranks that it earned an interesting, though by today's standards, rather inappropriate misnomer of 'The Yiddlesex Regiment'. Other regiments with a noticeable proportion of Jews within the ranks received nicknames such as 'The Royal Jewsaliers' and 'King David's Royal Rifle Corps'. Aby would have felt at home and at ease with his

Judaism. Indeed, he would not feel unabashed in asking for leave to celebrate the Jewish holidays.

So that he might serve the country he had come to think of as his own, Aby gave his name as Harris (as we have already seen), and his nationality as British. It also appears he gave his age, not as nineteen, but eighteen. Perhaps the recruitment office calculated that upon completion of training, he would have attained those 'vital' nineteen years, and signed him up on that premise.

Aby joined the Army without Joseph or Rebecca's consent and to quote Sylvia Pankhurst, 'they were bowed down with sorrow when he disclosed it'. There is no evidence however, that they tried to 'claim him out' as underage, as did the father of Joseph Rosenbloom.

Young Rosenbloom gave his account of underage service in the March 1916 edition of the Jews' Free School magazine. The editor's intention was for the boy's story to act as a deterrent to other would-be underage soldiers, but his account of derring-do probably only fuelled the fires even more. His account, under the title 'The History of 14 months Soldiering' bears full reproduction. Joseph was only fourteen when he went to war.

Dear Readers,

The Editor has asked me to tell my old school-fellows a few of my experiences in the army.

Well, I joined the London Welsh Regiment in September 1914, when I was 13 years and 9 months old. Before a month passed, I found myself being 'claimed' out by my father, but in 24 hours I was in the Army again. This time I joined the Essex Regiment and no one knew I had joined again. The next morning I went to Stratford, and from there to Warley. Here they gave me a suit of khaki, and a complete kit.

After two days' rest at Warley, they sent me on garrison duty. Day after day we did drills with the rifle and physical exercises. At the end of six months we were fit for service. One day the Colonel came round asking for volunteers for the front; I was one who volunteered with 49 other *men*. The next morning I bade my friends goodbye and departed. We arrived at Plymouth at 3 o'clock, and joined the 29th Division. We were all put on a troop ship and sailed the same day.

We passed Gibraltar, Malta, Egypt, Lemnos, and Imbros, a Greek harbour five miles from the firing line. When we arrived near Turkish soil, the bullets and shrapnel were dropping all around us. After a few hours' fierce fighting we got firmly set on land. The Royal Naval Division, many of them young lads, brought up ammunition to us in the firing line.

For a fourteen-year-old to comment on the youth of the 'powder monkeys', they must have been very young indeed.

The day we landed was April 25th, 1915, a day that will never be forgotten by any soldier who was in it. A few days passed by and nothing happened, except the Turks made a few counter-attacks. Then one day we made a great charge, for the purpose of taking Achi Baba, but we failed. We gained about six miles along the line, and the Turks lost heavily. We were burying Turks 50 at a time in the trenches we captured from them.

It was quiet for the next five weeks, only for a few counter-attacks, which always failed, with heavy losses. June 6th, 1915, was the day when we made a charge in which I was wounded. I thought my last day had come. I fell unconscious when I was hit, and when I opened my eyes again, I was at Egypt, in Alexandria. I was blind for three weeks, and I thought I had lost my sight, but thank God I regained it. I came out of the trenches on the 6th of June and was back again the 3rd July. I soon became familiar with the trenches again. I had a very narrow escape on 6th of August, when we made a great charge. We had helmets on, on account of the heat of the sun. A bullet went through the top of my helmet, and escaped my head by an eighth of an inch. Another bullet hit my left shoulder, but luckily did not go through.

After this charge we had to stand on dead Turks, to fire over the parapet. Later on we went to Sulva Bay, on the extreme left. There we lay until I was notified by the War Office. My father had been after me again. On November 2nd I went on a mine sweeper and that took me to Lemnos. There I was put on a cattle boat and in three days arrived in Egypt. We had a little trouble during the voyage with a submarine. Another week passed and we found ourselves in the Bay of Biscay.

On 27th January we were in dear old England once again. We arrived at Plymouth, and that same day I was in Warley once again. I found Warley was the same old Depot, with the same Recruiting Sergeants. On the 30th of Jan. I was supplied with ordinary clothes, and I was a civilian once again. I came home, and my father, who had tried hard to get me out, and succeeded, was happy to see my face again. Now I am at work, and think seriously I had better stick to it.

I may say that although I was discharged on account of the untrue statement I made about my age, I left the Army with a very good character from my Commanding Officer, a fact I shall always remember with pride.

With best wishes to you all,

Yours sincerely,

Joseph Rosenbloom.

The 11th Battalion of the Middlesex Regiment was raised on 8 August 1914 when three officers and twelve NCOs of the 1st Battalion arrived at Inglis Barracks, Mill Hill (the Regimental Depot of the Middlesex Regiment) from the base at Woolwich. These fifteen men formed the nucleus of the new battalion and were joined by another three officers and twelve NCOs from the 4th Middlesex three days later. A number of retired warrant officers returned to the colours, receiving new warrants at their old rank. Both the Regimental Sergeant Major (RSM) and the Regimental Quartermaster Sergeant (RQMS), often known in army slang as the 'Quarter Bloke', were appointed in this way. With the recruitment machinery well oiled and honed to military perfection, the whole Battalion was recruited in a week, and training programmes maintained the impetus.

About a fortnight after the Battalion first came into being they were on the move, for the first time, as a whole entity. They went by train to Colchester where they joined the 12th Division of Kitchener's First Army (known with typical army pragmatism as K1) then under the command of Major General J. Spens, CB. Here old men and officers of the Regiment continued to join and a real *esprit de corps* took hold of the new battalion. For others, their initial steps into the Battalion were still via the Depot at Mill Hill. Aby was one of those who joined at Mill Hill, as was another young man by the name of Arthur Redford.

Arthur Redford enlisted on 23 August 1914. It is possible he just scraped in before the Battalion embarked for Colchester, but it is equally likely that he shared accommodation and transport to

Colchester with Aby where they would have joined the rest of the recruits. A tall, thin twenty-five-year-old, Arthur had been a motor racer prior to joining up. His previous military experience in India with the Nagpur Volunteer Regiment from 1909 until 1912 (when he came to England) was apparently recognized, for he was immediately appointed as Lance Corporal. It seems clear that his educational and family background also led him to be marked early as a suitable candidate for a commission. Whether at this time Arthur and Aby knew each other as more than ships that pass in the night is unknown, but later Arthur Redford did indeed come to know Aby.

Major W.D. Ingle was appointed to command the 11th Middlesex, and Lieutenant L.L. Pargiter was made Adjutant. Both were to survive the War, not entirely unscathed, and both were to have a bearing on Aby's fate. Meanwhile, Joseph and Rebecca Bevistein and Aby's much loved sister Kate anxiously took up every letter he sent them, and evidence suggests he wrote very often. In almost every letter 'the lad expressed regret for the grief and anxiety he had caused his parents, and concern for their happiness'. This last quote is from Sylvia Pankhurst, who was afforded the opportunity of reading more of Aby's letters than we have note of today.

Despite the efficiency of the British Army in terms of logistics and organization, it was completely overwhelmed by the massive swell of recruits, the first hundred thousand being signed up within a fortnight of Kitchener's call.

The Rev. P. Middleton Brumwell, Chaplain to the 12th Division and later, compiler of the published Divisional history, said the following.

> Training in the elements of drill and route marching commenced at once; but rifles and implements of war were not forthcoming to equip such large numbers, and improvised wooden rifles were used therefore to accustom the recruits to the handling of arms.

There was simply not enough accommodation, nowhere near as many uniforms and weapons as were required and more importantly, a shortage of suitable officers and NCOs to train these recruits into becoming efficient soldiers. Ever pragmatic, the solution was to turn Britain into a vast campsite, and to issue the men with a mish mash of old uniforms and equipment – or in many cases, require them to train in the clothing they joined up in.

One soldier of many, having to make do in his own clothing, was Henry Bolton, a private with the 1ˢᵗ Battalion, East Surrey Regiment.

> We were generally handicapped by shortage of rifles and equipment, for I was doing my first two months training in the clothes I enlisted in. I received my first suit of khaki (and that a second hand one) in the last week of November, my rifle about three weeks after that and then another suit the week before Christmas, this time I had a new tunic and old trousers.

As far as officers and drill sergeants were concerned, many retired soldiers, commissioned and enlisted, returned to the colours in their country's hour of need. As honourable as their intentions no doubt were, some were not up to the job, but with a desperate need for experienced officers and NCOs at the front, they would simply have to do their best.

In a letter to his wife dated 15 September 1914, a private of the 8ᵗʰ Royal Sussex Regiment touched on the issue of instructors.

> One of the most pitiful things here is the incompetence of our instructors. They are nearly all illiterate and most have been out of the Army some 10 years. One slouches about in a bowler hat and confesses he does not understand some of the drills. The Company Sergeant-Major is a weak, stupid fellow, looks 55 or 60, doesn't know his business.

There is reason to suppose the 11ᵗʰ Middlesex fared more favourably than some battalions, in that its compliment of officers were all drawn from regular battalions or were newly commissioned. As already mentioned, some senior NCOs were re-enlisted or re-warranted men, and on the matter of training, Everard Wyrall, the contemporary author of the Regiment's Great War history had a comment.

> With experienced officers and formed of the splendid fighting material which was forthcoming in August, 1914, and the early days of the war, the Battalion soon engaged in vigorous training.

It is probably safest to say that the 11ᵗʰ Middlesex, like others, had a compliment of officers and NCOs covering a wide range of competency. It must also be borne in mind that it is all too easy for enlisted men to find fault in those put in charge of their destinies. Nevertheless, there are many accounts of urgent need calling into service those who had already earned their rest. They had to conduct training as best they could, and with woefully out-of-date field manuals.

Training was geared more to raising the physical fitness of the men and boys, and nodded infrequently towards the practicalities of the war they would soon enter. Soldiers were drilled and went on route marches. They went on cross-country runs. They drilled some more, and once in a while they would get to practise bayonet charges, and would go to the ranges.

Aby served with B Company of the 11ᵗʰ Middlesex later in the War, and although inter-company transfer was not uncommon, there is no evidence to suggest he served with any other. It is likely he trained, as did Henry Bolton, in his own clothes, or perhaps in one of the blue serge uniforms that were widely issued to recruits of the New Armies. Drills, physical training, handling of arms with either a wooden rifle or a relic from a time gone by and route marches would have been his lot. That, and the never-ending task of cleaning kit. Blanco. Soldier's Friend. Spit and polish.

For two months the Battalion remained at Colchester, and as one of the country's main garrison towns, we may assume (but not with any sense of confidence) that accommodation was somewhat better than the many tented camps that sprang up in parks, playgrounds and open spaces throughout the country. With the infrastructure well established it is also likely that food may have been better than the men of less permanent accommodations had to endure. There are conflicting accounts of the quality of army food during this period, ranging from quite inedible, to tasty and satisfying. Weekend leave was frequent with travel passes being issued for the journey to and from home by train. When there was no leave, or to fill in the gaps between such periods, contact with home was by one of the most efficient postal services in existence at the time – that of the British Army.

In October 1914, by now fit if not fully equipped, Aby proceeded by train with the Battalion and the rest of 36 Brigade to St Martin's Plane, Shorncliffe where they almost certainly spent a month under canvass. Aby shared the deprivations of life in a tent during an inces-santly wet autumn with his comrades until November when the

45

Brigade moved into a hutted camp at Sandling. Here they stayed, almost until the end of 1914 when they moved once again, this time to billets in Folkestone. It was at about this time that Lieutenant Pargiter signed the discharge papers for Lance Corporal Arthur Redford, a procedure necessitated by his intention to accept a commission. He received a temporary commission on 7 November 1914, but Second Lieutenant Redford was not to sever his links with the old battalion.

Lieutenant Colonel Ingle set up Battalion HQ at the Westcliff Hotel and the Battalion remained at Folkestone for the next three months. Then on 20 February, the Battalion set off on a long route march, carrying full kit and equipment – less ammunition – from Folkestone to Aldershot, a distance close to a hundred miles. Now in a proper khaki uniform, carrying the famous SMLE rifle, Aby must have shared a feeling of pride with his comrades as they marched in Brigade and Division. As George Coppard explains, they did not rush.

> The march was done in easy stages and took nine days. At East Grinstead we marched past Sir Archibald Hunter, GOC Aldershot Command. The next day Lord Kitchener became the highlight on our journey.

George admitted to feelings of anticipation in actually laying eyes on Kitchener, but as in many things, the reality did not match his high expectation.

> In his greatcoat Kitchener looked very big, but so baggy and grey – nothing like the dark handsome posters of him which were displayed all over the country.

It is interesting to note a slight variation in the account of this march given in the Regimental history – at least in terms of duration. In that account it is stated that the march took five days with stopovers at Ashford, Maidstone, Edenbridge, Dorking and Guildford.

Nine days or five, the Division arrived footsore and weary to be billeted in Aldershot's red-bricked barracks which were functional if not quite as comfortable as the ones they had left at Folkestone and Hythe. After six months of hard training Aby must have been as fit as he ever had been, and ready to have the last of his civilian edges smoothed off. But he was still only eighteen by the Army's reckoning – and just sixteen in actual fact.

The original plan was for the recruits to be ready for action after six months' training, but six months came and went and the New Army had no word of when they might expect to join an army in the field of action. The Battalion kept up its training, and the men drilled and practised rifle firing. They peeled potatoes and cleaned their uniforms, polishing buttons and applying Blanco to webbing. In their spare time the men would play cards – Brag, Pontoon, or Crown and Anchor – and go on forays into Aldershot town, or watch the nightly variety turns that were put on in the canteen. Beer could be got at tuppence a pint, pianos were played and men sang. But everyone knew this could not last forever and soon the Battalion would cross over into France. Soon they would be at the front.

In March 1915, command of the 12th (Eastern) Division passed from Major General Spens to Major General F.D.V. Wing, CB, CMG. Rumours of a move to the front must have increased around the end of April – a week or so after Aby's 17th birthday – for Aby was told that when the Battalion moved out, he was to be left behind. The most logical reason for this decision was that he was still, in the Army's estimation, a matter of weeks short of the required nineteen years of age. Aby begged to be allowed to remain with his comrades and battalion, and following a spell of leave he wrote home, reminding his mother not to forget his '19th' birthday. Was he preparing her lest an officer of his battalion contact her for confirmatory details? It certainly seems very unlikely that a son would have to remind his mother of the exact details of his nativity.

Dear Mother,
    I arrived safe and everything is all right. I was very sorry to leave you, and very sorry to see you cry so much as you did, but never mind, I will come home one day, so be happy at home. Dear Mother, do not forget my 19th birthday, that is on Saturday, 1st May. I want you to enjoy yourself on Saturday. Dear Mother, I did not like to leave you on Tuesday. I was very sorry to see you cry. Tell Father and Kate to be happy ...
From your loving son, Aby.

Dear Mother, I would like your photo to hold on me.

The last line perhaps indicates that Aby realized departure was imminent, and that separation from his family would be real. The sea would soon separate him from them, and they would be more than a mere train-journey away. Aby's letters to his mother Rebecca have come down to us through their publication by Sylvia Pankhurst in circumstances that will be explained later. It is at the same time fortunate they have survived in this form, yet frustrating that hardly any of Aby's letters are quoted in full.

There could be no doubt as to the reality of an imminent departure to the front when the enlisted men were ordered to have their heads shorn and were then issued with acid so that anything that shone, such as buttons, cap badges and shoulder titles, could be dulled down. As George Coppard reports, it was an issue that appealed to the men – almost an order to break the rules.

> Never was there such speed into putting an order into effect. Even the blades of our bayonets did not escape the tarnishing process, for nothing that might glint or gleam in the sunlight was exempt from the prohibition. Surely this was the most revolutionary order given in the British Army. The lads fairly howled with delight as 'Soldier's Friend' was flung away by the hundredweight. 'If that's how they bleedin' well want it, that's how their bleedin' well going to get it,' remarked one wag.

Saturday, 1 May 1915 quickly came and went, and Aby was now officially, if not actually, nineteen years old. There may have been reasons other than his age why Aby was going to be left at the barracks. We cannot know. We do know that whatever the reasons, Aby overcame them, for he did indeed stay with his battalion.

On 31 May, Aby penned the last letter he was ever to write in England. As a general rule, it would be wrong to make firm conclusions from a letter alone, because the writer always has an intention. For example, a writer may harbour emotions he wishes to conceal from his correspondent, and easily achieves this in what he chooses either to include or omit. Here however, it is easy to detect the nervous boy inside the soldier.

> My Dear Mother, Father and Kate.
> I am going to the front today. We go to Folkestone, and from there on ship to France. As soon as I get there I will send

you a letter. Dear Mother, I am very sorry I could not see you all before I go away, but be happy all the time I am out. If I have luck I will come home. Dear Mother, as I am writing this letter to you I am trying to be happy myself. Tell Nick I am going to the front.

Is 'Nick' the boy who had lived two doors down from Aby and who was for a short time his schoolmate? It is highly possible, and bordering on probable. Aby continues:

Give my best love to all the people in the street. Always think of me, Mother, and I will think of you, but don't cry, be happy. Good-bye, Father and Kate – Your loving brother, Aby.

Aby was one of the 11th Middlesex Battalion's 785 other ranks and twenty-seven officers who boarded one of two trains waiting at Government Siding at Aldershot. The first left at 8.20 pm and the other at 8.55 pm to arrive at Folkestone at 11.45 pm and 1.15 am respectively. It was certainly a rush for the occupants of the second train, for they embarked upon their ship – the SS *Princess Victoria* – at 1.30 am.

The *Princess Victoria* was a small steamer, just 1,096 tons, more used to the Stranraer to Larne run as part of the fleet owned by the Portpatrick & Wigtownshire Railway Committee. Launched in 1912 it saw service as a troopship for the duration of the war. Two other ships with the same name sank. One sank in the Humber in 1940 after striking a mine with the loss of thirty-six lives. In the 1950s another *Princess Victoria* capsized in a gale and 134 people lost their lives. It is ironic to think that although Aby's *Princess Victoria* evaded the U-boats and was never sunk, it carried many, many more men to their deaths. It was eventually scrapped in 1934.

At 3.00 am on 1 June 1915, the *Princess Victoria* arrived at Boulogne and the Battalion disembarked. Aby, and the 11th Middlesex, had entered the War.

Chapter 6

Men for Flags

In our heart of hearts believing
Victory crowns the just,
And that braggarts must
Surely bite the dust,
Press we to the field ungrieving,
In our heart of hearts believing
Victory crowns the just.

Thomas Hardy

How did Aby fit into the Middlesex Regiment, and how did the 11th Battalion fit into the British Army? It is intended that this chapter will provide the reader with basic information about the armies of Europe at the outbreak of the War, details of how the British Army was organized and finally, a little about the history of the regiment Aby joined.

At the outbreak of the War, the British Army was tiny in comparison with those of the other major powers. Indeed, it was so small that the Germans called it 'that contemptible little Army', an insult soldiers took and turned into a label of pride worn by those 'old contemptibles'. The British Regular Army, including its reserve forces, stood at about 235,000 men. Compare this with France's 700,000, Germany's 840,000 and Russia's 1.3 million. To widen the gap still further, all the powers except Britain could call up vast numbers of conscripts, Germany being able to field up to five million men, and that just for starters.

Britain was unique among the major powers in having no conscription and only the Territorials in addition to the various components of the Regular Army. At the outbreak of war, there were

50

fourteen territorial divisions and fourteen territorial cavalry brigades, all highly trained and organized along the lines of the Regular Army, but intended for home defence. Small it may well have been, but the British Army was perfectly formed and envied for the professionalism and training of its soldiers.

A day after war was declared, Field Marshal Earl Kitchener of Khartoum was appointed Secretary of State for War, and on that same day he asked Parliament to authorize an augmentation of the Army to the tune of half-a-million men. Kitchener was not one of the majority who believed that it would 'all be over by Christmas' and he set to prepare for an affair that he thought likely to draw out for a period of some three years. On 11 August 1914 his famous proclamation went out calling for 100,000 men between the ages of nineteen and thirty to come and give General Service 'for a period of 3 years or until the war is concluded'. Within two weeks the required number of men had volunteered.

The new men were mustered into battalions named after sixty-nine existing regiments and distinguished by sequential numbering and the addition of the bracketed word 'Service'. Most battalions were made up of two regular battalions and a reserve battalion that 'fed' the other two. One regular battalion would be for home service and the other one for duties abroad.

As an example of the naming of battalions, let us look at the Norfolk Regiment. Before the War there were 1ˢᵗ and 2ⁿᵈ Battalions, the Norfolk Regiment. One of the New Army battalions serving with Aby's 12ᵗʰ Division was the 7ᵗʰ (Service) Battalion, the Norfolk Regiment. Many battalions had so many Service or New Army battalions added, that the designations reached well into the twenties and sometimes thirties.

The first hundred thousand men to volunteer provided sufficient manpower to field an additional five divisions and these went into service collectively as the First New Army – later shortened to Kitchener's Army and then simply 'K1'.

What about Army organization and lines of command? Aby was a private soldier, answerable only for himself and with nobody to command. So long as he attended to his private concerns, which were to maintain all disciplines applicable to him, he would be seen as properly discharging his duties. He was one of roughly 1,000 men attached to the 11ᵗʰ (Service) Battalion, the Middlesex Regiment.

Although the battalion was the basic unit of an army, the battalion itself was organized into manageable sections; the 'Section' being the smallest unit, not including a half-section or a patrol made up of a varying number of men according to its mission. At full strength a section was made up of fourteen men with a corporal in charge.

Four sections made up a platoon, which was usually commanded by a second lieutenant assisted by sergeants. A full lieutenant would command some platoons, and a major who was second in command of the battalion may have had a platoon of his own.

Four platoons together formed a company which was commanded by a captain who would have some five officers and 150 men at his disposal.

Four companies (named A, B, C and D) made up a full battalion, which was commanded by a lieutenant colonel, assisted by a major as second-in-command and an adjutant, usually with the rank of captain. He was the administrative mainstay of the battalion together with the quartermaster who could be a senior lieutenant or captain.

At the beginning of the War and right up until early in 1918, four battalions were 'brigaded' together forming a brigade under the command of a brigadier general. After that time only three battalions made up a brigade. These days the British Army calls a brigade commander 'Brigadier'. The rank has lost the term 'General' and also the badges of rank associated with generalship, although the American equivalent is still a 'one-star' or brigadier general and a brigadier is entitled to display a star on his or her official transport.

Three infantry brigades together with artillery, pioneers and sappers, medical, veterinary, and cavalry units, were brought together to form a division commanded by a major general. A division was fully self-sufficient and was in effect a mini-army. In earlier times a varying number of divisions formed an army, but so huge were the numbers involved in modern warfare that an intermediate grouping was found necessary and divisions were gathered into corps, which were led by a lieutenant general. It may appear strange to some that although a major outranks a lieutenant, a major general is actually a grade lower than a lieutenant general. This is a throw back to the seventeenth century when the full name of the lower grade was 'Sergeant Major General'.

An army was made up of a number of corps and was commanded by a full general answerable only to the General Officer

Commanding the British Expeditionary Force, who held the rank of Field Marshal. From the beginning of hostilities until shortly after the Battle of Loos, this was Field Marshal Viscount French. After Loos, Douglas Haig replaced him.

So, Aby served in the 11th (Service) Battalion, the Middlesex Regiment, which was part of 36 Infantry Brigade. Together with 35 and 37 Infantry Brigades, and various other units, these formed the 12th (Eastern) Division.

At the outbreak of the War there were eight Regular Army divisions. New Army divisions were numbered sequentially and the earlier ones (and a few later) given a title, such as 'Eastern', 'Western', 'Irish' or 'Light'.

There was little time for pomp or ceremony in the New Army battalions – they had no dress uniforms or other ceremonial accoutrements – but they carried their regimental names with pride. Aby was a 'Die Hard' and his cap badge was the same as that worn by the Regular Army battalions of the 'Die Hards', or Middlesex Regiment. Like all British Army regiments, the Middlesex had been through several name changes. Initially, regiments were known officially only by numbers. On formation there were two regiments that would eventually amalgamate to form the Middlesex and these were the 57th and 77th Regiments of Foot. Later these would become the West Middlesex and East Middlesex Regiments respectively. By the time of the First World War these two regiments had already joined, and were known officially as the 1st and 2nd Battalions, Duke of Cambridge's Own (Middlesex) Regiment. But through many changes the officers and men of the Regiment thought of themselves as the 'Die Hards'.

The term 'die hard' has a general application, and is applied to those who refuse to budge despite the odds, or to a stubborn breed who stick at it when others may have eased off or given up altogether. It is a term well known and often used, but the Middlesex had it first. There can be few other regimental nicknames that have become part of the English language. It was earned during the Peninsula War at the Battle of Albuhera on 16 May 1811.

Colonel Inglis was the Commanding Officer of the 57th Foot. He was leading his men, who he called the Fighting Villains, when he was mortally wounded by grapeshot, being struck in the neck and chest. He would not allow anyone to take him to the rear where he could have received treatment, but ordered them to lay him close to the front where he called on encouragement to his soldiers. When the fight was at its peak he shouted, 'Die hard the 57th, die hard!' The men of the 57th obeyed their commander's last order. The casualties were horrendous with the loss of 420 out of 570 enlisted men and twenty out of thirty officers. 'Our dead,' said Marshal General Lord William Beresford in his dispatch, 'particularly the 57th Regiment, were lying as they fought in their ranks, every wound in front.'

The colours of the Regiment were thereafter to carry the battle honour 'Albuhera', and the name was also enscrolled on the cap badge, but it was the term given to them by other soldiers – The Die Hards – of which they were most proud. There was (and still is) an intense rivalry between regiments, so to be given such praise by another was praise indeed. Colonel Inglis's name was immortalized by naming the Regimental Depot at Mill Hill after him, and at the time of writing it is still known as Inglis Barracks more than thirty years after the Regiment ceased to be and close to 200 years after its namesake's death.

The Die Hards have a history of which to be proud. In Aby's war, the 4th Battalion fought with such courage in the opening hours of the Battle of Mons, that the Germans raised a memorial to them at St Symphorien Cemetery, calling them the 'Royal Middlesex Regiment'. It is rare indeed to have a memorial erected by an enemy. By the end of the War, ninety-three battle honours had been granted to the Middlesex Regiment and five Middlesex men had won the Victoria Cross.

Aby had joined a fine regiment, and now it was time for the 11th Battalion to join the fray.

Chapter 7

Somewhere in France

For it's Tommy this, an' Tommy that, an' Tommy wait outside;
But it's Special train for Atkins when the trooper's on the tide.
                                                    Rudyard Kipling

Major General F.D.V. Wing had commanded the 12th Division for a little over two months when he led it into France. A Royal Artilleryman, he was commissioned a year after the Zulu War and served with distinction throughout the Boer War achieving the rank of Brevet Lieutenant Colonel by its conclusion. He had commanded the artillery of the 3rd Division during the Battle of Mons and was present throughout the retreat, during which he greatly distinguished himself, leading to his promotion to Major General and ultimately his command of the 12th. He was possessed of a keen, personal interest in the welfare of his men, and in the months to come it would be an unusual day if he did not visit them in the front line trenches. He cared for the men of the 12th, and they came to hold him in great respect.

We have seen how the Army was organized, but what did it look like? How was Aby dressed? What equipment did he carry when he stepped off the *Princess Victoria* and what insignia marked him out as a 12th Division man? During the night crossing and when he disembarked at 3.00 am on 1 June 1915, he would no doubt have been thankful for his army issue long drawers and long-sleeved vest. His heavy, grey flannel shirt had its long tails tucked into olive drab (known incorrectly as khaki) woollen serge trousers that had provision for the wearing of braces, and vertical slash pockets in the side seams. His jacket, of the same rough cloth as the trousers, was of hip-length, four pocketed and buttoned up to the neck. It had a row of five large buttons, formerly polished to a sheen, but now acid-dulled and yellow-brown. Thick woollen socks served to cushion the impact of the leather of his hobnailed B5 ammunition boots, which were made rough-side out and undyed. By now used to their application, his puttees, again made of wool, were worn tightly wound from boot-ankle to just under his knees.

Old soldiers often despaired at their younger colleagues' first efforts to come to grips with puttees. Fred Wood reports how such an old Boer War veteran saved them from their ignorance.

> Some chaps had them tied from ankle to knees, others wound them round and round their calves like bandages. We were saved by an older man who had served in the Boer War, who showed us the trick. They were awful things.

For headgear, Aby had been issued with the standard 1902 pattern service dress cap. We know this from his photograph, but other colleagues may have worn the trench cap with the ear flaps known as the 'Gor Blimey', which started to appear in 1914. He neither wore, nor carried among his equipment, the famous steel helmet affectionately known as the 'battle bowler'. That piece of kit, estimated to have saved many thousands of troops from shrapnel injuries, was not to be widely issued until Aby's part in the War was over. Soldiers fought in soft cloth, peaked caps for the first two years of the War.

Albeit a night crossing and probably a little chilly on deck, Aby was probably not wearing his greatcoat, carrying it instead in his main pack. Soldiers of the New Army carried 1914 pattern leather infantry equipment, differentiating them from the regular and territorial soldiers who, for the most part, were still equipped with 1908 webbing. This was not a hard and fast rule, for it was not uncommon for units to be equipped with a mixture of the old and new. Uniformity took second place to practicality while there was a war on and the Quarter Bloke would make use of what he could.

The 1914 pattern equipment centred on a wide, brown leather belt clipped at the front with an 'S' buckle. It was fitted with two large ammo pouches, shoulder straps that crossed at the back and sufficient attachments to take a haversack, bayonet, entrenching tool and waterbottle. The main pack was fitted to the back, and a haversack was worn on the left side. Both were made of heavy-duty canvass.

Each ammo pouch contained fifty rounds of .303 ball ammunition in a cotton bandoleer.

Within this array, arranged in full marching configuration, Aby carried a black-gripped jack-knife, a mess tin, and a cloth 'wash roll' containing his razor, toothbrush, lather-brush, comb and cutlery. Also, two pairs of socks, a spare shirt and drawers. Finally there would be his 'iron ration' – never to be dipped into without orders. This comprised a tin of bully beef, dry biscuits and a ration of tea and sugar.

Aby was armed with a Short Magazine Lee Enfield rifle, .303 calibre, in the butt of which was a whipcord pull-through for cleaning the barrel and a small bottle of oil. About his person he wore his official soldier's disc and carried his paybook.

There was not a lot of space left for personal equipment or keepsakes, but most soldiers found somewhere to stow precious reminders of home or loved ones. Each man carried everything he needed, and George Coppard, just a few months older than Aby, put it like this:

> Like a tortoise my home was on my back. My pockets bulged with bits and pieces. It was not easy trying to grow to manhood loaded like a pack animal.

A New Army man was almost at once identifiable as such from the various cloth insignia sewn onto his uniform, on the sleeves or under the back of the jacket below the collar. Various shapes (squares, triangles or discs for example) would indicate a man's brigade, and the colour of the shape would show his battalion. These were evident as soon as the New Army men landed in France, and later in the War divisional insignia also began to be used on uniforms, as well as on transport vehicles and ambulances.

The divisional emblem usually took the form of a cloth patch worn at the top of the left sleeve and bearing a simple design instantly recognizable and not easily confused with any other. For example, the 9th (Scottish) Division wore a circular patch bearing the likeness of a thistle, the 10th (Irish) Division, a narrow green stripe, and so on. Major General Wing's men were identifiable by the representation of the Ace of Spades. It would not be long before they thought of it as a shovel for digging and repairing trenches. There was another, rather more unfortunate connotation – at least for the French. From time to time, local people would appear very wary of the men from the 12th.

It transpired that the Ace of Spades emblem was also known in the French Army, where it signified a body of men of doubtful character who had been enlisted from prison.

Once off the *Princess Victoria*, the men of the 11th Middlesex were formed up at Boulogne Harbour and marched two miles to Ostrahove Large Camp where by 4.30 am they were all settled in. Later that day, Jacques LeCoutre was posted to the Battalion as interpreter.

The Battalion were allowed the remainder of the day to rest from their travels and the following morning to prepare for more. At just after midday the 11th were on the march again, this time covering four miles to the railway station at Pont de Bricques. Here the troops were entrained, leaving for Wizernes, twenty-seven miles to the east as the crow flies, and just south-west of St Omer. It was a cause of some hilarity that the trucks in which the men travelled were marked '40 Hommes, 8 Chevaux'. Aby could not know; those same words would greet another generation of Jews as a prelude to the greatest horror of the twentieth century, when similar trucks were used to carry them off to concentration camps.

The 11th arrived at 6.30 pm and then marched a further one and a half miles to their billets at Gondardennes. Here they were to have their first experience of many to come concerning the unsuitability of billets. Thankfully all other units were settled in, but Transport found their billets to be wholly unsuitable for the basic needs of their animals. Horses and mules had to be picketed on a brick courtyard. Picketing was not accomplished until 11.30 pm with many a picketing peg breaking on the hard surface.

While Transport solved their problems, Aby and the rest of the 11th Middlesex got down to the important business of eating. Rations per man, as laid down by military regulations, were generous especially when considering the privations many an East End boy endured at home. The official ration was 1½ pounds of fresh or 1 pound of salted meat, 1 pound of biscuit or flour, 4 ounces of bacon, 3 ounces of cheese, ½ pound of tea, 4 ounces of jam, 3 ounces of sugar, 2 ounces of dried or 8 ounces of fresh vegetables, 2 ounces of tobacco and ½ a gill of rum (undiluted) per day. It does not look too bad on paper, but alas, paper was often as close as a soldier came to receiving his stipulated ration.

And what did Aby think of the bacon, whenever it managed to appear? What about the nature of the rest of the food? Were provisions made for the dietary needs of the large number of Jewish soldiers serving in the New Armies? At the beginning, there were very few efforts made to ensure a kosher diet. In all fairness, it was as much as could be done to provide food at all, let alone kosher food. That is not to say there was none at all, for of the 3,475 British Army chaplains serving in August 1914, sixteen were Jewish and there is evidence that Jewish chaplains made efforts to secure a more appropriate diet for 'sons of the word'. Ironically, it appears that at least some Jewish lads rather liked bacon and complained when it was replaced by something more suitable as a result of a Jewish chaplain's efforts.

We do not know how strictly Aby tried to stick to a kosher diet. We know he celebrated Jewish holidays and that his family regularly attended *Shul*, but we also know he did not habitually wear the skull cap or *teffilin*, so it can be safely assumed that the kosherness of his food was not a problem for him. Apart from anything else, there was a dispensation applicable to these circumstances, so Aby and his Jewish comrades could eat without fear for their souls, even should they be strictly observant.

Aby's problem with food, in line with the rest of British soldiery, would have been the lack of variety and quantity, if not so much now, then certainly while they were at the front. Staples during the War included tins of bully beef, Maconochie's 'dinner in a tin' and a particularly unpopular plum and apple jam made by a company called 'Tickler'. In common with other unpopular aspects of the War such as whizz-bangs and sergeant majors, Tickler's jam was immortalized in song, as the following ditty shows.

> Tickler's jam, Tickler's jam,
> How I love old Tickler's jam,
> Plum and apple in a one pound pot,
> Sent from Blighty in a ten ton lot.
> Every night when I'm asleep,
> I'm dreaming that I am,
> Forcing my way through the Dardanelles,
> With a ton of Tickler's jam.

On the subject of billets, they varied from comfortably cosy to virtually intolerable. Sometimes the men were fortunate indeed and they were billeted in the cottages of local people where they were made welcome, their rations augmented by whatever the occupants had to offer. Aby was to experience the generosity of local folk and was to write of it in one of his letters home.

> Dear Mother, you don't know how they like English people. What they have to eat they give you – don't matter how poor they are.

One has to wonder at the content of Aby's letters, for some were written when times were very bad for the Battalion, yet Aby's letters mention little of hardship. One is left to assume that he preferred to keep these things from his family knowing that they were already worried about him and not wishing to increase their fears. On the other hand, perhaps he believed that any talk of hardship, except in the most general of terms, would fail to get past the censorship of the platoon officer. Certainly, he often asked for money in order to supplement his diet with locally available fare.

Good billets were everything a soldier could wish for. Bad billets on the other hand, could be very bad indeed and offer no comfort and little shelter. There are reports of men being billeted upon local people who resented them and charged vastly inflated prices for stale beer and mouldy food. Draughty barns and derelict buildings were often employed for the job, but even these were better than no billets at all. Often, staff personnel, who were responsible for arranging billets, did not perform their duties in the most efficient of manners, and soldiers exhausted from a stint at the front would find their allotted billets occupied by another battalion, or that the space available was nowhere near sufficient.

A word in defence of the much maligned staff officers; their task was immense. Imagine thousands of men moving daily, from trench, to reserve, to billet; route marches, changes of arrangement with short notice. It is easy to speak ill of the man in whose steps you have not had to tread. In any case, staff officers were the subjects of numerous contemporary maledictions; we need hardly supplement them so long after the logistical problems they struggled to control.

The Battalion stayed at their Gondardennes billets for another two days, but the time for resting had ended and the days were filled with a variety of drills and exercises to further prepare the men for trench warfare. The Battalion had a practice route march; they trained at rapid manipulation of their rifle bolts and practised signalling by use of buzzers. Naturally, their kit was inspected and they also sat through lectures on the recognition and significance of French and German uniforms and insignia. They were trained to limber-up and unhook draught animals, by day and also by night, and they went through instructions on trench assault organization. Meanwhile the Battalion signallers connected telephone wires between Battalion HQ and the four Company HQs, as well as to Brigade HQ. All good practice for the days to come.

At 12.30 pm on 4 June, the now Captain, Adjutant Pargiter, received a heads-up that the Battalion must be ready to march off at 7.00 am on the following morning. Official orders to the same effect arrived at 1.20 am.

In common with the preceding days, 5 June 1915 was a hot one. The Battalion marched with the rest of 36 Brigade in full marching order. In a recently published book, an author has this to say on the subject of marching.

A society in which any distance of more than a mile is an occasion for getting out the car can scarcely conceive that a march of twenty miles carrying seventy pounds or so, is no great hardship for trained troops.

Here is what Captain Pargiter had to say about the march on 5 June.

The Battalion marched off at 7 am and proceeded 15 miles to bivouacs ¾ mile North of CINQ RUES (1 mile West of HAZEBROUCK). Very hot and dusty. 173 men fell out. It is considered that the weight of the pack is too heavy.

The underlying theme of the modern, well researched work, whose author is a former officer of the British Army, is that a large section of the public needs their preconceived ideas about the First World War challenged and their illusions shattered. He reasons that it is virtually impossible for the modern Briton 'even to begin to understand what the war was like'. There is indeed much truth in this, but nevertheless it sits uneasy to read a modern reference that is intended to detract from the horrors and deprivations of that period. It would hardly be surprising to learn, should such evidence come to light, that during his army days, the author led his well fed, well equipped and physically fit modern soldiers on marches probably exceeding twenty miles, and with heavier packs, but in this – and other examples we shall see later – perhaps it is better to listen to a voice from the time.

It is not just the civilian population who sometimes fails to understand the realities of scale and endurance experienced by Tommy. Former soldiers who may have fared well in conditions approaching, but well short of those in the Great War, sometimes err in the opposite direction.

Marching on such a hot and dusty day, on the French *pavé* roads with their large cobbles, wearing the thick woollen uniforms and carrying that 70lb pack, Aby and the others had a very uncomfortable time of it. Lance Corporal Mountfort of the 10th Battalion, Royal Fusiliers described his experience of a similar route march.

> We marched fifteen miles on Wednesday. It doesn't sound much, but when you think of the heat of the day, the weight of the packs and the state of the French roads you will understand it was an amazing strain on our endurance. The French roads are horrible. Through every village and for a mile or two each side they are composed of great rough cobblestones, about 8 inches square and not over carefully laid. Apart from the unevenness there is the difficulty that the nails of our boots step on them as on ice. If two villages are only a few miles apart the cobble stones carry on and join up the two, so that they stretch for miles. Our packs I cannot find words to describe. It is a cruel, unnatural weight that no man should be called upon to carry.

As part of a New Army division, it is quite likely the men tried to keep up their spirits and sang as they marched. This was a pastime not at all prevalent (although not entirely absent either) among pre-war regulars, many of whom thought it rather silly and a waste of good wind that could best be conserved for when it was needed.

One highlight of Aby's day appears to have been the sighting of an airship 'seen a long way away (20 miles approximately) to North-West, approximately about YPRES'. This was a time when any man-made airborne contraption was guaranteed to attract maximum attention. However, there is not much doubt that the true highlight was to reach journey's end where Aby was able to remove his boots in the fields of Les Cinq Rues where he was bivouacked. One hopes he was able to dip his feet into a cooling stream.

By 6.00 am the next morning the boots were back on and the Battalion was on the march again, this time with eleven miles to cover. At 10.00 am the column passed through Merris where General Sir William Pulteney inspected it. Onward and past the General, the day grew hotter and the road was as dusty as it had been on the previous day. Three men fell out because of the heat, one of whom was admitted to hospital and the others received treatment and short respite at the 37th Field Ambulance.

The Battalion reached Noote Boom at 11.30 am and the men were assigned billets. Now Aby was very close to the front; in fact, a mere two-hour march away and close enough for the CO to mount an inlaying picket of platoon strength and to send out patrols along two roads from the west. The following day it was again, very hot, but at least there was no marching to be done. The day was spent in rest and reorganization. The picket was increased to company strength and men were found for three patrols. Duties were much the same for the following day, 8 June, but at 1.00 pm the weather broke and there was an unusually arid thunderstorm, which lasted until 3.00 pm. It passed, leaving the weather much more comfortable than the preceding days.

While the 11th Middlesex sheltered from the storm, more noisy than wet, the regular soldiers of 19 Infantry Brigade (part of the 2nd Division) were sheltering from shrapnel and a great deal of sniper action, in trenches with which Aby was soon to become familiar.

The Battalion was now on final countdown to its first encounter with the enemy and its first taste of trench warfare. Like schoolboys who approached those end of term exams and crammed in some last minute study, Aby and the others went through final instructions before the real thing. With the sound of medium and heavy artillery clearly audible, every man must have harboured fleeting, or not so fleeting, thoughts of his own mortality, kept for the most part to himself and masked by the usual banter and forced cheerfulness.

Officers were sent up to reconnoitre the approach to Armentieres – the town that acted as the very pale beyond which there were Germans. If the 11th, as a battalion, was to receive a final pep talk, the time was now. George Coppard recalled his battalion receiving not so much a pep talk, as a warning of dire consequences should any man not come up to scratch. The CO addressed his men on the day before they entered the trenches for the first time.

> He reminded us that we were on a war footing and that the severest military laws would apply for any dereliction of duty, such as desertion, mutiny, leaving the trenches without permission, cowardice and sleeping while on sentry duty. A conviction by court martial for any such offence would carry the death sentence.

Following Lieutenant Colonel Warden's grim words, Captain R.A.M. Bassett, the Adjutant of the 6th Queen's (Royal West Surrey Regiment), made the event even more jolly by reading out the names of the men who had been executed, thirty-two of them for military offences.

> I was stupefied as the adjutant droned out each man's name, rank, unit and offence, followed in each case by the words 'and the sentence was duly carried out'.

At 5.00 am, 10 June, the 11th – less transport and a guard of twenty-five men – marched towards Armentieres. They were inspected by yet another high ranking officer – this time Brigadier General the Honourable F. Gordon, CB, DSO commanding 19 Infantry Brigade. Just as a taster for things to come, it rained heavily for two hours during the march.

At 9.00 pm, twenty-four hours before Aby's first operational deployment, parties of officers and NCOs from the 11th joined the regulars from the 1st Middlesex and the 2nd Royal Welsh Fusiliers in the trenches for instruction in trench warfare and routine. The remainder of the Battalion settled into billets. The next day it was to be their turn.

Two companies of the 11th proceeded to the trenches at 9.00 pm on the 11th, for twenty-four hours' instruction. The allotted period elapsed without serious incident, and the remaining two companies relieved those already in the trenches to start their own twenty-four hour stint. It was two C Company men who became the Battalion's first casualties. One received only slight wounds and stayed on duty. The other had to be removed to the casualty clearing hospital at Bailleul, six miles to the north-west.

For the next three days, the system of rotating the pairs of companies – twenty-four hours in the trenches, twenty-four out – was to
continue with no more casualties suffered until the 15th. It was Aby's
company that was to suffer the first fatality. Lance Corporal W.H.
Batten from B Company died of wounds he had received in action on
15 June and was buried at Erquinghem. Two other B Company men
were wounded and evacuated to Bailleul.

In British army life, the battalion could be compared to your own
little community – your own street. You knew everyone in it, if not
by name then certainly by appearance. The loss of anyone from your
battalion, in those early encounters, was an event worthy of notice.
Continuing the analogy, the men of your own platoon were brothers,
known by name, by temperament and by all those little nuances and
habits that come to be known through living together, come sunshine,
come rain. If the men of your platoon were brothers, then men of the
same company were cousins. Aby then, had lost a brother or a cousin
in those opening days of the War, with two more receiving serious
wounds. The savage bite of war's reality had drawn blood.

At 3.15 pm on the 15th, the Battalion marched by route back
to their billets at Noote Boom into which they settled at 6.40 pm,
each man with at least a taste of life in the trenches and all with new
experiences to ponder in those moments before sleep. Aby and B
Company especially, had accumulated much food for thought with
the loss of their comrade.

The 11th Middlesex had learnt a little of the protocols involved
in trench life and now they were allowed a few days respite to consolidate. There were classes given over the next nine days and the
men stayed in the same billets. Perhaps at this point it would be
pertinent for us to learn a little about the look, feel and organization
of the trenches.

At this time in the history of the War the trenches stretched from
the Belgian coast near Ostend for over 400 miles running in a roughly south-easterly direction into the south of the Alsace region,
stopping at Switzerland. Not even a year into the War, the whole
ethos of military tactics had changed, and while far too many
general officers clung to their outdated manuals and relied too heavily on lessons they had learnt in India and Africa, innovation and
adaptation were very much in evidence at the sharp end. The
mechanics of fighting had changed so quickly and to such an extent,
that a soldier involved in the retreat from Mons in August 1914 who

received a temporary 'Blighty' one, would have been at a complete loss if he returned to war in 1916. What had started as a war of cavalry charges, close ordered troops under the voice command of their officers and a series of manoeuvres and contacts with the enemy, had become a war of mechanical devices of horrendous destructive power, mines and bombs. Modern weaponry laughed in the face of old tactics.

The modern soldier could fire consecutive aimed shots more than three times faster than his Napoleonic counterpart and five times further. The capabilities of artillery from this period, when compared to that of Wellington's army, was nothing short of phenomenal. Despite the horror they were to become, trenches were a good idea to begin with, perhaps the only option that would protect men from the machines. Flesh and blood could no longer withstand an attack into such a storm of lead and steel, so the digging of trenches began. Following the failure of conventional tactics against efficient weaponry, it was a case of dig or die, where no one expected these field works to be anything more than a stop-gap in a temporary stalemate. The fact that it was actually a case of dig *and* die was to be realized all too quickly. Following three months of frenetic manoeuvring and fighting, serious digging-in began in November 1914.

To describe the standard British trench system of the day, it is best to start with no-man's land; that strip of terror that separated the trench systems of the opposing armies. Ranging from anything between twenty yards wide, which was not common, to almost a thousand, the usual width of no-man's land was anything between 200 and 500 yards. Both sides made extensive use of barbed wire, not merely stringing it at random like a steel cobweb, but in a tactical manner with the aim of slowing down an enemy advance and channelling them into positions of high vulnerability to rifle and machine-gun fire.

The trench closest to the enemy was known as the front line or more correctly, the firing line. Seen from above this was not just one long, straight, continuous ditch but had a crenellated form to minimize the blast from any shells that scored a direct hit. Every eighteen to thirty feet, the direction of the trench would change at a right angle, usually to the rear but sometimes forward to provide flanking fire. The trench would then revert back to its original direction and the pattern repeated. Every few hundred yards along the firing line, or as frequently or infrequently as was necessary, a narrow, shallow trench was dug forward leading to an isolated, short trench known as a sap. These would serve as forward observation areas, head-starts for patrols or machine-gun pits. Close behind the firing line – between ten and twenty yards – was the narrow command trench. Little more than a communication trench, its purpose, as the name suggests, was to provide a means whereby the sector commander could rapidly move to any part of his command. Here was the most likely location for a forward position of Battalion HQ and the officer's dugout.

Between 200 and 500 yards to the rear of the firing line was another line, constructed in the same way and connected by communication trenches. This was the support line, in place to provide a second line of defence, and further back still was the reserve trench from where a counter-attack would be launched should the enemy succeed in breaching the forward defences.

Each line of trenches had its own cookhouses, first aid posts and latrines. The firing and support lines had machine-gun pits. With communication trenches zigzagging at frequent intervals, blind alleys and saps, it became necessary to identify each individual component of the trench system by name, and it became customary to dub them with cosy sounding street names. Aby was to become familiar with 'Devon Lane', the 'New Cut', 'Dugdale Road', 'Brewery Corner' and 'Vigo Street'. Sometimes they were named after a local event, such as 'Sniper Alley'.

In plan the trench was narrow at the bottom and ideally planked with sufficient space underneath to serve as drainage. A man was supposed to be able to walk upright without becoming vulnerable to fire, but this appeared to be based on a premise that soldiers were all no taller than 5' 6" and there are many accounts of men being sniped in the head because they were too tall for the design and forgot to duck. The trench walls were revetted, or cladded, wherever possible to prevent them from caving in during wet weather. Materials used were many and varied, depending on what was available. Brushwood, old doors and wire mesh were all used, but as the War progressed, sheets of corrugated iron increasingly began to fulfil the role. The forward wall had a fire-step cut into it just under two feet up from the base level giving defenders the means to stand in a firing position with their rifles clearing the parapet. The parapet was made of compacted soil extending forward of the trench for four to five feet. It allowed a man to fire his rifle clear of ground level while affording him protection from incoming fire. Another band of earth, the parados, extended rearward from the back wall of the trench and served to protect the defenders from shell bursts. It could also, of course, serve as a parapet should the enemy manage to get to the rear of the trench. Sometimes sortie steps were cut into the leading wall. These were little more than footholds reinforced with a brick or short piece of planking, and their purpose was to facilitate exit from the trench for patrols or wiring parties.

British trench systems varied from those of the enemy in several ways in terms of materials used and construction. The most notable difference was the lack of protection British trenches gave against overhead shell bursts. The Germans had deep bunkers and often their dugouts were reinforced with concrete. The British enlisted man had to make do with a funk hole, which was nothing more than a scrape two feet into the trench's forward wall, lined with groundsheets. These were prone to collapse, sometimes burying their occupants alive.

This then, gives an impression of the trenches at their best, and indeed, some systems may have appeared just so in the early days. But by the time Aby came to them, the early days had long since passed by.

Chapter 8

From Ploegsteert Wood to Loos

If I were fierce, and bald, and short of breath,
I'd live with the scarlet Majors at the Base.
Siegfried Sassoon

Aby was back in his Noote Boom billet by 6.40 pm on 16 June 1915. The Battalion had lost one man killed and four wounded, and although the men now had experience of the trenches and could honestly say they had 'been to the front', their tour had officially been only for training and familiarization. They were yet to hold part of the line in their own right without regulars from 19 Infantry Brigade overseeing them. For the next week the Middlesex men licked their wounds and embarked upon more training. There was instruction in the use of the machine-gun and other classes. On 18 June a reinforcing draft of a sergeant, a corporal and sixty-three other ranks joined, and they too were quickly subsumed into the rounds of class work and drill.

On Wednesday, 23 June 1916 General Luigi Cardorna launched his Italian army against Austro-Hungary. Completely outgunned in artillery and machine-guns, 60,000 Italian soldiers were to lose their lives in the first week of the offensive. Back within our own theatre of war, the officers of the 11th Middlesex went north, crossing the French/Belgian border, to the trenches occupied by the 8th Battalion, Worcestershire Regiment. These ran north-east of Hill 63 at Ploegsteert Wood. The officers familiarized themselves with the trench systems and made preparations for the takeover while the men remained back at billets taking in their last classes. The next day the Battalion marched out at 5.00 am arriving at Ploegsteert Wood three and a half hours later where they were to lay up in heavy rain for the rest of the day. Once again, nature was adding to the discomfort of the men, just as they prepared to take the line.

The Ace of Spades Division began taking over from the 48th (South Midlands) Division at 6.00 pm. It soon became apparent that the outgoing battalions, all of the Territorial Force, had left the trenches in an appalling condition. They were 'very muddy and dirty, [and] apparently had not been cleaned up at all for weeks'.

Aby's brigade – the 36th – took over from the left and George Coppard's – the 37th – from the right, while 35 Brigade was posted as reserve on the GHQ line as the trench was known. At 11.00 pm the takeover was complete and Aby shared the dubious honour, with the rest of the 11th Middlesex, the 6th Queen's and the 6th Buffs, of being the first of the New Army men to occupy the front line. Almost immediately the Battalion suffered one man wounded.

Lieutenant Colonel Ingle set up Battalion HQ in Ash House. The following day another Middlesex man died of wounds, and Battalion Staff had a narrow escape when a shell blew the roof off their newly established HQ. Aby's first full posting to the front was a fairly quiet one. A war diary for one of the 12th Division regiments for this period says: 'Except for thirty high-explosive shells fired at our trenches, the day was quiet.' George Coppard notes that Ploegsteert was commonly called 'Plug-Street' by the Tommies and mentions this posting in his book, *With a Machine Gun to Cambrai.*

Here we had our first taste of German artillery fire. The first indication was the sound of four deep booms, which seemed to come from well behind the enemy lines. In a few moments I became aware of pulsating rushing sounds, increasing in power and intensity. The threatening noise struck equally between my ears, and I knew instinctively that shells were heading in my general direction. The final vicious swipes of the projectiles as they rushed to earth turned my stomach over with fear, which quickly vanished when four hefty explosions occurred in some ruined houses a hundred yards to the rear.

Aby's posting ended when the 2nd Canadian Regiment relieved the Battalion. Relief began at 8.30 pm but not without mishap, for a Canadian accidentally shot another of Aby's comrades and yet another was hurt in a separate accident. The last of the Middlesex were out of the trenches by 11.30 pm when they formed up and marched to Oosthove Farm where the whole Battalion was billeted.

It was now time for Aby to learn one of the realities of life at the front. Periods of rest were not always as restful as the men may have wished. Working parties had to be formed by day and by night, and classes were maintained. It was not unusual for men to be worked harder during periods of rest than when they were actually on the firing line. Frank Birkinshaw, a sixteen-year-old private serving with the Royal Warwickshire Regiment, wrote home about it in May 1915.

> We are relieved tonight and go back for four days rest. I think it must be a little joke to call it rest, for we do twice as much work as in the trenches.

Admittedly, Frank was talking about a spell in the reserve trenches, but even when further back from the lines and in proper billets, there were tasks that needed doing and working parties to be found. Perhaps this is what kept Aby from writing as much as he usually did, for a lapse in hearing from him caused Rebecca much concern and made her sick with worry.

On Thursday, 1 July 1915 the Battalion's strength was augmented by another draft, this time of sixty enlisted men, bringing the full compliment to thirty-one officers and 1,009 other ranks. The following night Aby received a letter from his mother and wrote back at once to put her mind at ease.

> Dear Mother
> I received your letter on Friday night. I have been in the trenches four times and come out safe.

Aby includes the Battalion's visits to the trenches that formed part of their familiarization posting. But then why should he not? The trenches were just as muddy, just as smelly, had to be endured for twenty-four-hour periods and for one of Aby's NCOs, they proved to be equally as deadly.

> We are going in again this week. Dear Mother, we go in the trenches for six days and then we get relieved for six days' rest. We get 4s 2d every two weeks. When I get my money I buy

bread and other things. It is very dear and the money does not last very long. I also buy some cigarettes. We had to be in the trenches on Saturday and Sunday nights. It seems very funny to think that it is Sunday in the trenches. Dear Mother, I do not like the trenches. I think you know that I would like to ask you if you can send me some money to buy things if you can send it. You write you was nearly going mad. You know it takes two days to get to London, or more.

The following day was *Shabbat*, but far from being able to observe the traditions, Aby was off to the trenches again. The trenches were by no means uniform throughout the entire front. In chalky areas drainage was usually sufficient to keep them at least bearable, but even these became difficult after heavy rain, as testified by Second Lieutenant Kenneth Macardle of the 17th Battalion, Manchester Regiment.

We left those Mericourt trenches yesterday. It was a pretty wood but the trenches were very wet in the rain and crumbled in a good deal – in fact in the relief two men had to be dragged out of the slush by force from above, so hopelessly did they get stuck up to their thighs in sucking sloppy mud.

In boggy areas and those with less permeable soil types, a little rain went a long, long way. Unfortunately for Aby, he was in trenches of the latter kind. Sometimes the water table was so high that it was completely impractical to dig down too far, and so trenches had to be built up. These were known as box-trenches and were made by piling up soil ramparts and augmenting them with whatever was to hand. They were very unpopular as their line was only too obvious to the enemy, and soldiers would often prefer to dig down into the near-liquid mud rather than present such a clear target to enemy artillery.

The 12th Division had extended towards the south-east having taken over from regulars of the 27th. They now held the line from Ploegsteert to the River Lys. On Saturday, 3 July the 11th Middlesex relieved the 9th Royal Fusiliers (with whom they were brigaded) and began an eventful seven days in the trenches. Headquarters were set up at Despierre Farm. Once again the trenches were found to be in a bad state of repair. The parapets had worn thin in places and were not bullet proof, as a number of men would learn at the cost of their lives. One man was killed and another wounded on the first day of their tour. The next day, Sunday 4th, they lost another two; forty-year-old Private Thomas Nodder from Davenport and Private W. Rogers.

Now becoming familiar with the routines of trench life and perhaps feeling the need to avenge their losses, the Middlesex began to become more adventurous and mounted several small operations against the enemy. By the time they were relieved by the 6th East Kent Regiment (The Buffs) six days later, they had lost five men killed by high explosive shells and sniper fire, but the general feeling was that they had gained superiority over the enemy. On the first night the Middlesex mounted a four-man patrol into no-man's land led by Captain H.G. Hill. They reached the enemy wire before being fired upon. They returned fire and withdrew to friendly trenches.

Lieutenant Colonel Ingle and Battalion Staff again had a lucky escape when their headquarters were attacked by artillery fire on 5 July. That night another patrol went out and this time got within twelve yards of the enemy wire. Patrols were mounted every night and on that of the 9/10 July, Sergeant Campbell shot two enemy soldiers. Lance Corporal Watson killed another and Private Penny broke nine enemy periscopes and shot one enemy.

The 11th also had some success in dealing with enemy snipers, and one of Aby's NCOs, Lance Corporal Hagley (who volunteered for every patrol sent out), shot one during this tour. A persistent and very active, red-haired German sniper who the men had nicknamed 'Rudolf' was also hit, this time by C Company's sergeant major, CSM Bently. Corporal Sullivan did a lot of sniping over the parapets and is thought to have killed two Germans. On Thursday, 8 July the Battalion was to suffer its first officer casualty when Captain Hill, who had led the first patrol, was wounded in the neck and shoulder.

There were also acts of bravery during this tour, such as when on the 5th, three men working at a saphead came under fire from the enemy at a range of seventy yards. Nineteen-year-old Private Danny Sullivan, another East End lad like Aby, was shot and killed. The other two men at the sap (Sergeant Murphy and Private Tompkins), not wanting to leave the lad, brought him back to the main trenches under heavy fire. Danny was later buried at the Calvaire Military Cemetery.

On the last night in the trenches a star shell set the parapet alight and No. 618 Private Smith leapt up on to the parapet under heavy fire putting out the flames with his hands.

Another man who drew the attention of his officer and of enemy machine-gun fire was No. 188 Private Bristowe who approached an old dugout a few yards from the trenches where it had been rumoured the enemy had occupied. He went up to the dugout making a noise by banging empty tin cans together. In reply came machine-gun fire.

Part of the line had been harried by enemy machine-gun fire from a team set up in a cart. To assist a battery of the Royal Field Artillery to zero in on it, Sergeant Lewonski climbed up on to the parapet in full view of the enemy whose trenches were only twenty-five yards away, and fired several rounds at the cart. Captain Pargiter commended the Sergeant for his good work in this incident and for his sniping work at the parapet.

Following relief on Saturday, 10 July, the Battalion marched to billets at Pont de Nieppe just over a mile to the north-west of Armentieres. One C Company officer had the sad duty of writing to Mary Ann Sullivan of 26 Buxton Street, Mile End to tell her that her son Daniel had been killed. Meanwhile, Aby did not waste any time before writing home again. It appears Rebecca had learnt from a neighbour that they received an allowance from their soldier-son, and had asked Aby about it in her last letter.

> You want to know why you don't get any money; it is because I never signed a paper saying that I want to allow you 6d a day – it is too late now … Dear Mother, I know it is very hard for you to miss me from home, but still, never mind, be happy and don't cry. I think you know I am very sorry I done that, but if I have luck I will come home. How is father getting on? How is yourself? Do not be afraid to write to tell me how you are getting on.

Once again, there are frustrating gaps and omissions that were not relevant to the purposes of the original publisher, but quite enough to show that Aby made light of his experiences. Apart from mentioning the need for money to buy more food and cigarettes, his words always appear to have the aim of putting his mother's mind at ease. It looks like he was fortunate enough to secure a good billet at Pont de Nieppe, and a parcel from home.

> Dear Mother, when we come out of the trenches we stayed in the people's houses. When the parcel came and I opened it they cried and said: 'What a good mother!'

74

Aby showed his hosts the photograph of Rebecca that he carried with him.

They looked at your photo. 'Poor mother,' they said.

The people Aby stayed with were poor enough themselves, but they gave Aby some of what they had to eat. A comfortable billet and a full belly was good for morale, and it appears Aby was even able to get a thorough, albeit cold, bath. Bathing arrangements may have been rather primitive. It appears the River Lys may well have served as Aby's bath, as it did for George Coppard.

A bathing parade was organised before we returned to the trenches, and we marched to Pont de Nieppe and bathed in the River Lys … In the warm summer evening we sported in the water like kids without a care. The war seemed far off, yet the line was but a mile away.

After two days at Pont de Nieppe, the 11th left their transport section and proceeded to billets in Armentieres. It can be seen from the account so far that a pattern of trench life is emerging which is somewhat different from the popular impression. Arrive in France, march to the trenches, and stay there until you are wounded, killed, made ineffective by disease or the War ends. Not quite the case as Aby himself explained to his mother in his letter dated 2 July. A battalion would take over a section of the line for four to seven days during which time companies would take turns at the firing line – usually not exceeding twenty-four hours – and the rest of the tour would be spent in the support trenches. The men would then be moved to the reserve trenches or be relieved by another battalion when they would proceed to billets for rest, or more usually to form working parties.

Working parties were required for a variety of tasks, usually involving hard physical work. Aby's battalion were required to provide so many working parties over the course of the following months that Captain Pargiter was to complain, raising the matter with the Royal Army Medical Corps on the grounds that their health was suffering through lack of proper rest.

'What's a soldier for, Dad?' goes the old story.

'For hanging things on,' replies his father.

Parties were needed for re-wiring, carrying heavy iron screw-pickets and rolls of barbed wire, repairing trenches, digging new ones and sometimes for roles equally as taxing as firing line duty. In September 1915, Private Edgar Foreman (Civil Service Rifles) described such a duty in a letter home.

When we were in reserve our whole Company had to form a covering party to another Battalion, who came up to dig a new fire-trench at night-time. As soon as it was dark we went out in front until we were midway between the German and English trenches, where we lay down at about 20 paces interval between each pair of us: the first night we were by ourselves at 10 paces. Our job was to form a screen so that the working party could not be surprised. We were there from 8 to 2 am. The first night was the most exciting, the Germans shelling our trenches and our artillery replying: we could hear the pieces from the shrapnel dropping all round us and a large number of stray shots whizzing through the long grass, it was the longest six hours I have ever spent, but the only casualties in our party were an officer and a private who were shot by our own men mistaking them for Germans; they were both killed.

In Armentieres, the 11th Middlesex rested and attended classes, then on the third day out of the line they had to provide men for working parties, one of whom, Private F. Austin, was killed. Working parties were required on the next day, and the next and the one after that, bringing our lads up neatly to their next spell 'down the line'. Before they relieved the 9th Royal Fusiliers in trenches 81 to 84, they lost their leader, if only temporarily, for Lieutenant Colonel William Ingle was admitted to hospital with suspected appendicitis. Major W.C. Newton took command.

It was quiet in the trenches the next day, but at 8.30 pm strange lights appeared in the night sky. Two hours after completing the takeover from the 9th Royal Fusiliers on 21 July, 'a yellow light was seen high up in the air at a distance of approximately three to four miles to the south east of our trenches'. The mysterious light appeared for a few minutes then vanished, followed by the launching of three white rockets from the German trenches to the north-east. This sequence was repeated several times, and all the while the wind blew gently from the south. Later, an enlisted man was wounded.

The 22nd was another uneventful day except for the man who was wounded, and for the rain that began at 4.00 pm and continued all through the night. On the third day of this tour, some Middlesex men found the range of the enemy. A sniper and a man in a German working party were believed shot by two C Company men, and twenty-three-year-old Captain Mills accounted for another man in an enemy working party. Later that evening, Second Lieutenant Leach led a patrol so close to enemy lines that the enemy could be heard talking. At 9.00 pm, there were more strange goings-on in the sky when a cigar-shaped airship passed under a bright moon. Now it was the turn of D Company to count coup on the enemy and a small patrol made up of three lance corporals and three privates patrolled up to the enemy trenches.

The enemy proved to be very active on the 24th making much use of snipers and shelling the communications trenches. Two men were killed and five wounded. Lance Corporal Collins was taking a party of sick men down the communications trench known as Wessex Avenue when a shell burst wounded him in five places. Two of the sick party were also hit, and the Corporal took them to the dressing station and returned to the trench looking for any others who may have been hurt before getting his own wounds dressed.

It was on this day that the 11th Middlesex suffered its first officer fatality when Second Lieutenant Harold George Hawkins of Crouch Hall Road, Hornsey, London, was sniped in the head while on the firing line. Typical of many men killed in this way, he was doomed from the instant he was hit, but did not die at once. He was taken to the 36th Field Ambulance where he died of the wound. The twenty-four-year-old son of Francis Henry and Lydia Hawkins was buried at Cite Bonjean Cemetery after a short service given by 36 Brigade Chaplain, Captain C.C.T. (Cuthbert Charles Trewhitt) Naters. George Coppard lost a good friend to the same cause, and his graphic description of the event highlights the horror that is often overlooked when a man is described merely as having been shot.

Lulled by the quietness, someone is foolish and carelessly lingers with his head above the top of the parapet. Then like a puppet whose strings have suddenly snapped, he crashes to the bottom of the trench. There is no gradual falling over, but instant collapse.

Moving on from general terms, George goes on to talk of his friend.

> The fire was going nicely and the bacon was sizzling. I was sitting on the firestep. Just as I was about to tuck in, Bill crashed to the ground. I'll never forget the sound of that shot as it found its billet ... A moment before, Bill had been talking to us, and now, there he was, breathing slightly, but otherwise motionless ... The battalion doctor was in attendance at the first-aid post. 'He can't last long,' he said, and so we left Bill who died later that morning. When we got back to the front line we [Marshall and I] were both ravenous with hunger. My bacon and bread was on the fire-step, but covered with dirt and pieces of Bill's brain. I inspected the front of my tunic and trousers and there were more bits there: my boots were sticky with blood.

Later, during the night of the 24th, one of Aby's NCOs – Lance Corporal Percy Bence – led two other B Company men on a patrol to within fifty yards of enemy trenches. The following day, an enemy machine-gun in the trenches opposite D Company was located and 'silenced' and for the first time Harry Hughes-Jones led a patrol across no-man's land. Second Lieutenant Hughes-Jones's name appears often in the Battalion's War Diary; he appears to have developed a flair for leading forays towards the enemy. The twenty-six-year-old was born in the vicarage at Pembroke and was the son of the Rev. Isaac Hughes-Jones. Before the War he had been 'studying for the bar'. Though destined to become a barrister he was not unfamiliar with military matters. He had qualified in musketry in April 1912 while he was a cadet sergeant in the Infantry Unit of the Oxford University Contingent of the Territorials.

On 26 July, A Company's Sergeant Higinbottom led Lance Corporal Beatty, Private William Garland and Private Mills on a bombing party across to the enemy. Between them they landed eleven bombs into the enemy trenches. Later on in the day, the same sergeant led a second party, this time throwing six bombs and managing to evade those thrown back by the Germans.

None of the Battalion were killed on this day, but twenty-three-year-old Lance Corporal Percy Porter from Buxton in Derbyshire died of wounds. The following day – the last in the trenches for this tour – Private T. Manning also died of wounds at

1. Aby, aged 13.   *(Courtesy of Betty Jacobs)*

2. The Bevistein family, circa
   1911, on the occasion of
   Aby's bar mitzvah.
   (Courtesy of Betty Jacobs)

3. Aby's school as it is today
(May 2004).

4. No. 11/1799 Private Abraham Harris, 11th (Service) Battalion, The Duke of Cambridge's Own (Middlesex) Regiment. *(Courtesy of Betty Jacobs)*

5. Josh Maguire as Aby.
   *(Courtesy of Simon Rawles
   {photographer} and
   Testimony Films)*

6. Josh Maguire as Aby.
   *(Courtesy of Simon Rawles
   {photographer} and
   Testimony Films)*

7. Preparing to shoot a trench scene for *Britain's Boy Soldiers*.   *(Courtesy of Elizabeth Cosslett {photographer} and Testimony Films)*

8. The farmhouse where Aby was arrested as it is today (May 2004).

9. Taken from close to Aby's place of execution, looking towards Sailly Labourse. This is the road the firing party took.

Headquarters,

    12th Division.

                 With reference to the attached Proceedings
of Field General Court Martial,-

                 I recommend that the sentence of Death
on Private CARTER, 11th Battn. Middlesex Regiment be put into
execution.

                 He was one of a number of men of the
11th Middlesex Regt. who left the trenches without permission
while a severe engagement was on.   The Battalion was so disorga-
nised that I ordered patrols of another battalion to search the
cellars in VERMELLES on March 5th. to arrest all men of the 11th
Middlesex Regt. found hiding there.   These men were afterwards
sent to SAILLY.

                 Five of the worst cases were selected for
trial by F.G.C.M.   There were numerous delays and four out of the
five men became effective.

                 The discipline of the battalion is not
good, and I think it is necessary to make an example of this man.

                                     Brigadier General,

                    Commanding 36th Infantry Brigade.

13/4/16.

10. Copy of the recommendation for the execution of Private Henry Carter, 11th
Battalion, Middlesex Regiment. The document shows the handwritten comment
of Field Marshal Douglas Haig. *(With the permission of The National Archives)*

11. Aby's headstone. It shows his name incorrectly spelt, and his age as twenty.
(*Courtesy of Elizabeth Cosslett, {photographer}*)

12. Memorial to the Fusiliers of Vingré.

the Field Ambulance. The 11th Middlesex had now served for fourteen full days and nights in the trenches and had sustained fourteen casualties dead.

One way or another it had been the Battalion's most eventful stint in the front line and they must have been pleased to be relieved by the 9th Royal Fusiliers. They made their way to billets in Armentieres. But once again, there was to be little rest for Aby or his colleagues. Working parties were required by day and by night. There were also guards to be mounted and brigade duties to complete.

Having had so little rest that the medical authorities took up the case, the 11th were back six nights later for their seventh tour in the trenches, completing the relief by 10.40 pm without a hitch. 'The night was wet and very dark,' writes Captain Pargiter.

Events were unfolding very typically for the 11th. This was very much a war of machine-guns, snipers, artillery and bombing raids. The bomb, or grenade, had surpassed the rifle as the principle weapon in trench warfare to the extent that an October 1915 publication recommended that every infantryman be trained in grenade use. Each platoon was to have an NCO and eight men picked from the very best soldiers to act as a standing establishment of bombers. General Headquarters had already released recommendations for the composition of a Trench Storming Party. It was to be led by an NCO and comprise fourteen or more men each fulfilling one of four functions. There were to be the bombers, the bomb carriers, the bayonet men and the sandbag men.

The first full day of the new tour was a quiet one for the 11th. Again, C Company's Second Lieutenant Hughes-Jones led a night patrol across no-man's land hoping to scout out enemy wiring, but there were too many German working parties out and they failed to get close enough to the wires.

The next day, 4 August 1915, the Germans were very active with rifle and machine-gun fire. Sergeant Higinbottom took a patrol so close to the enemy that they heard talking, and threw in seven bombs all of which exploded in the enemy trenches. Later, Captain Mills who had led a patrol during the last tour and was believed to have killed an enemy, was looking over the parapet when he was hit in the head by an enemy bullet. Like Second Lieutenant Hawkins and several men before him, he was taken to the Field Ambulance, but died the next day.

For the rest of the tour the 11th experienced shell fire from the enemy, by day and by night. To enable British artillery to fix the line of the parapet to assist in ranging the enemy, they fitted white sheets at the junctions of trenches. Several bombing raids were carried out and on the last day the enemy took to shelling the communications trenches wounding two men, but surprisingly, apart from Captain Mills, only one other man was killed. On 8 August at 8.30 pm, the 9th Royal Fusiliers began their relief of the 11th, and so the cycle of life in the trenches and in the billets continued. Once again, their much needed rest was seriously eroded by the never-ending need for working parties. One soldier, Private A. Smith, was accidentally killed on their first day of 'rest'.

> 9 officers & 592 other ranks [to be] found for working parties out of a total available strength of 560. This continual breaking in on to very necessary rest is causing great dissatisfaction, especially as in many cases the parties required by R.E. are too many for the work to be done. Also R.E. keep the parties waiting about unnecessarily. The health of the Battalion is suffering & the medical authorities have taken up the matter.

Whether and with whom the medical authorities took the matter up is not known. It is on record that working parties had to be found for every remaining day of the rest period. Aby and the 11th Middlesex, having completed twenty-one days in the trenches since arriving in France and having nearly every rest period interrupted by the need for working parties, were back in the trenches again, for their eighth tour. To make matters worse, this was to be their wettest, muddiest tour yet, and it would be several weeks before the Battalion were issued with waders.

The Battalion's War Diary entry for 16 August 1915 reads as follows.

> Heavy rain fell for two hours, from 12.30 pm till 2.30 pm. All trenches were flooded, in some places nearly 3 feet deep. A certain amount of water from the fire trenches flowed away but a lot had to be bailed out. Many dug-out floors under water. Enemy appears to have raised his parapet – noticeable especially opposite trench 84. Enemy active with machine-gun

fire. No enemy working parties noticed. One of our snipers believes he hit a German. No casualties.

The following day was once again dominated by the wet weather, although from the movement of smoke following a set route up and down the enemy line, Captain Pargiter deduced the presence of a light railway behind the German trenches. A patrol also went out and snipped off some enemy wire for closer examination. The War Diary entry for this day goes into quite some detail over the construction of the prize, stating it to be 'rather thicker than our wire'.

The next day, the Germans sent a wiring party into no-man's land which was dispersed by 11th Battalion machine-gun fire, and on 19 August, Second Lieutenant Leach took out a patrol of two men to the enemy lines near Les Quatre Hallots farm. They discovered the positions of two enemy listening posts. On returning from the patrol they threw bombs at one post and drew machine-gun fire. They reached British lines without casualty, although elsewhere in the trenches, the 11th suffered two casualties wounded.

During this tour the 11th Middlesex, so recently novices in trench warfare, were now acknowledged as experienced when they were assigned to instruct a newly arrived battalion, the 13th Royal Fusiliers.

On the last night of the tour an enemy patrol were seen approaching British trenches. 'A party went out & bombed them with, it is believed, good results.'

At last the 11th Middlesex, with the new boys of the 13th Royal Fusiliers in tow, were relieved by the 9th Royal Fusiliers and returned to billets at Houplines. It will come as no great surprise to hear that yet again working parties were required for every one of the five days rest. All too soon, and after receiving an equal number of casualties as had been incurred during their previous spell in the trenches, the 11th Middlesex were again relieving the 9th Royal Fusiliers. It does not take much imagination to realize how the men felt on that Thursday evening as they filed into the line, tired in body and spirit and with the prospect of another full tour ahead of them. At the very best they could expect days of boredom and discomfort. Their worst fears must have sat like lead in their stomachs.

At least the weather held on this occasion, and the enemy were quiet on 26 August – the night the 11th took over trenches 81 to 84 – and the cold of an August night was not likely to penetrate Aby's sturdy serge uniform. His uniform was not up to the job of protecting him fully from the extreme elements of a winter in the trenches, but then very little in its day was. The uniforms were probably about as good as they could have been for their day, keeping the men wrapped up in layers of flannel and thick wool. Of course, nothing was quite capable of keeping out muddy trench water, but it is interesting to note that the boots with which Aby was issued (and no doubt he spent much time greasing them), were more efficient at the job than those issued to British soldiers during the Falklands War sixty-seven years later.

Could it be that the deprivation of rest was beginning to affect the men to the extent that some considered extreme measures to get out of the trenches? On the Friday, three men were wounded, one accidentally, and to make up for a quiet first night, the Germans were more active than usual in their machine-gun and rifle fire. It was a damp squib though, for the next day it was quiet again. A patrol of the 11[th,] on the other hand, impressed their temporary CO who wrote a report to the Brigade Major.

> Headquarters,
> 36th Infantry Brigade.
>
> I wish to bring the following to the notice of the G.O.C.
> On the night of 28/29 August a bombing party of 'D' Company 11th Middlesex Regt., was fired on by a heavy Machine-gun. The party consisted of Lieut. Anderson., No. 10366 Sergt Campbell., No. 770 Pte Phillips., No. 12141 Pte Lee. Sergt Campbell and Pte Phillips were wounded and Pte Lee failed to return to our lines and has not since been heard of. Lieut Anderson and Sergt Campbell (already wounded) between them carried Pte Phillips (badly wounded) about 50 yards when Sergt Campbell became exhausted and was obliged to lie down. Lieut Anderson himself carried Pte Phillips the rest of the way to our trenches, returning at once to bring Sergt Campbell which he also succeeded in accomplishing. He then went out again to search for Pte Lee but being unable to find him returned.
> I consider that the personal conduct of both Lieut Anderson and Sergt Campbell during this affair deserving of special

mention and beg to lay the matter before the G.O.C. for his consideration.

W.C. NEWTON. Major
Commanding 11th Middlesex Regiment.

Major C. Parsons replied.

> The G.O.C. is much pleased to hear the conduct of LIEUT ANDERSON and SERGT CAMPBELL on the occasion you mention and they should be informed of this. Their names should be entered on the Regimental Records and they will also be entered on the Special List kept in this office for reference and future action as occasion for bringing them to notice admits.

The names of Gavin Bullen Anderson and Frank Albert Campbell were placed on the list. Twenty-seven-year-old James Lee however, never was found. He has no known grave, his name being one of those on the Ploegsteert Memorial (Panel 8).

For all the activity that followed over the next few days – run-ins with enemy patrols, bombings and machine-gun fire – it is surprising that there were no more casualties, and the Battalion was relieved by its partner in this endless dance – the 9th Royal Fusiliers – on Wednesday, 1 September. They went to billets in Armentieres and for two days, perhaps because of the heavy rain that fell, no working parties were required of the 11th.

It must not be thought that rest meant what it said, even when there were no working parties to be filled. There were still daily parades and inspections, kit to be cleaned and uniform to be seen to. It was during the month of August that a briefly kindled pragmatism concerning the polishing of metal items was extinguished. Somebody of high rank decided it was time for dull buttons to sparkle again and as George Coppard explains, it was a most unwelcome development.

> The luxury of not having to waste time and energy in senseless drudgery was to end. I don't know how high up the scale of rank the order came from. Whoever it was ignored the lessons of military history, which taught that troops should at all times be as inconspicuous as possible. Could it be that top brass feared that they might lose proper control of the

troops unless they re-imposed the iron hand of 'Bull'? The polishing of brass gear in the trenches was the very negation of the superb camouflage of the khaki uniform. It was tantamount to deliberately discarding a natural protection. Looking at it today seems crazy, but that's how it was and we had to grin and bear it.

There was however, some time to spare, and it seems Aby's thoughts turned to the possibility of leave and a spell at home for the Jewish holiday of Yom Kippur. Writing on 4 September, he said:

I might be home for the Jewish holidays ... I have got a paper for the Chaplain to show the Captain.

Aby, as a private soldier, had no idea that circumstances would rob him of any chance of leave or that his battalion was shortly to play a part in a battle that was to cost the lives of 60,000 British soldiers.

On Tuesday, 7 September 1915 the time came round once again to take over the trenches from the 9th Royal Fusiliers, but before that the whole Battalion was to be inspected by General Sir H.C.J. Plumer, KCB. He was pleased with what he saw and told the 11th that every man held himself well and behaved like a soldier and that they were very good at rifle movements. Plumer was a full general and commanded the Second Army at the time, and with his praises fresh in their ears, it may have bolstered their morale a little and helped them to get through the first night. There was heavy sniping from the enemy around midnight. The following day the Battalion suffered two casualties, one killed.

On Thursday, 9 September some of Aby's B Company colleagues went out on a bombing raid. There were two B Company patrols, one under the lead of Sergeant Crocker and the other led by Corporal Pound. Both attacked and bombed German working parties.

On Sunday, 12 September, Aby, still in the trenches, wrote home.

Yes, dear Mother, it is a very long time since we have seen each other. For the New Year I think you will go to the Synagogue and pray for me to see you very soon.

Two days later the 9th Royal Fusiliers were trooping in and the 11th Middlesex out of those trenches and off to billets in Armentieres.

Once again, by day and by night, working parties were required for each and every moment right up until the 11th had to return to the trenches. This does not mean to say that every man from the Battalion incurred such duties on every night of rest, and we may safely assume that some rest was to be had and that Aby and the others would have found some time to visit the *estaminets* of Armentieres.

Armentieres is without a doubt the best known location of all from the First World War that is not prefaced by the phrase 'Battle of ...' Immortalized by the ubiquitous Tommy's song 'Mademoiselle from Armentieres' and resurrected in the Second World War by Flanagen & Allen's 'If a Grey-Haired Lady says "How's Yer Father"', there can be few who have not heard of it. It is difficult, once hearing the ribald nature of the earlier song and the implication of a past liaison in the second, not to form an impression of the town as one of unadulterated licensciousness where every *estaminet* offered 'a little extra upstairs'. No doubt some of them did, but for the most part the standard fare of *estaminets* – a half-way house between café and pub – was more than welcome. Beer, thin though it often was, and platefuls of fried eggs and fried potatoes, and the jovial comradeship of fellows, forced though it may have been, went a very long way to cheer men tired from the trenches. And for those who wanted that little extra, full-blown brothels were easy to find.

Aby was a youth, like so many of his comrades, and was no doubt subjected to the usual pressures of young manhood. But again, like many of his fellows, the evidence suggests he had a religious and moral upbringing that is more than likely to have dissuaded him from contemplating a commercial solution to his natural yearnings. Private Archie Surfleet of the 13th Battalion, East Yorks, kept a diary and had this to say on the subject.

> [T]here seems a danger that 'our war' may only be remembered as a series of drunken orgies interspersed with a few cases of rape and almost nightly immoral relations with every available French and Belgian female. This sort of picture is far from the truth. At times it was bloody terrifying but, as for sex, most of the females were too old or too tired doing a man's job to be interested. There were 'Red Lamps' in some of the bigger towns but they were, comparatively, little used. The propaganda against VD before we went out and later was good enough to

deter the vast majority of overseas soldiers and those who 'caught a dose' suffered so much in so many ways their misery killed the 'urge' and discretion usually triumphed.

Whether or not discretion triumphed for the men of the 11th Middlesex, it is to be hoped that they at least found some time to relax and remove themselves from thoughts of the trenches, for their next tour would bring them into the Battle of Loos.

Chapter 9

Wounds for Christmas

And the Bayonets' long teeth grinned;
Rabbles of Shells hooted and groaned;
And the Gas hissed.

Wilfred Owen

There was an unfortunate incident on the last day of rest when one of the men was accidentally wounded during bomb practice. On the following day – Sunday, 19 September 1915 – the 11th relieved the 9th Royal Fusiliers (as usual) in trenches 81 to 84 near Houplines (as usual). By now Aby would have known that there was no hope of leave for the Jewish holidays and New Year, but he would still have had no idea of the battle to come. Enlisted men did their daily duty and carried out their routines, and it would not have served any purpose to pre-warn them that soon they may have to 'go over the top'. However, the strange build up of bundles of straw in the trenches must have led to some questions. Straw was used to raise 'smoke-curtains', which were sometimes used to mask an attack.

For the first three days the weather was fine, the enemy quiet and there were no casualties except for Private T. Huggins who died of wounds. This was possibly the man who was hurt in the bombing accident, and it is interesting to note that his service number, 1786, was only thirteen short of Aby's, suggesting a similar joining date. On the 22nd though, the Germans shelled Houplines with heavy explosives all around Battalion HQ, for one and a quarter hours. Only four men were wounded, and apart from the shelling the day was again quiet, while the weather continued to hold out. On the 23rd, British artillery had a pop back and later Houplines was again the target of German gunners. There was no damage and casualties were nil.

On Friday the 24th, Battalion HQ received Battle Operation Order Number One, a two-page document detailing the part that had been assigned to the 11th Middlesex in what was to become known as the Battle of Loos. Pronounced 'Loss' by the French and 'Looz' by Tommies, it was to be one of the bloodiest battles of the entire War. Loos has come to be remembered as an utter failure, a callous waste of the lives of over 60,000 British and Commonwealth soldiers and the final nail in the coffin of the then General Officer Commanding, Field Marshal Sir John French. Perhaps it deserves to be remembered as the success it so nearly was and for the unbelievable courage shown under the worst of conditions by the men. This was the battle when those men and boys who were first to flock to the colours had the opportunity to show their mettle, and they were not found wanting. A major factor in the failure at Loos was that Field Marshal French insisted on keeping direct command of the reserves, and when they were needed, they were too far off to deliver the extra impetus that may well have carried the day. It has been said that success here would have ended the War, but a miss is as good as a mile and the War was to wear on for another three years.

The First Army was made up mostly of Kitchener's citizen soldiers and a few remaining divisions from the savagely mauled and depleted Regular Army. Aby's division, the 12th (Eastern), formed part of XI Corps under the command of Lieutenant General R.C.B. Haking, CB. Major General Wing still commanded the 12th Division and Brigadier General H.B. Borradaile led 36 Brigade. As we will see later, Aby is to provide us with a possible clue as to the regard in which the divisional commander was held.

Often described as the unwanted battle because of the reluctance of certain members of the General Staff to commit to a push they saw as premature, the battle was precipitated, at least in logistical terms, by the fact that ammunition supply had at last begun to catch up with demand. This allowed for artillery bombardment on a large scale, thus supporting political pressure to achieve a decisive advantage over the enemy prior to the onset of winter. The offensive was to consist of a main attack by the French (in the Champagne area) and a second attack along the line extending from Arras to La Bassee by the French Tenth Army under Foch and the British First Army under General Douglas Haig. There were to be three smaller attacks, one on the Aubers Ridge, one on the line just south of Armentieres and another in the Ypres salient.

To begin with, the 12th Division were fairly low on the Order of Battle, and now within the Second Army they did not play a prominent part. Their duty was to hold the line east and north of Armentieres. Together with every unit along almost the entire British front, they were to light the bundles of damp straw forward of the parapets so that a vast cloud of smoke would blind the enemy to troop movements and confuse them as to the true line of the offensive.

By 11.30 pm on 24 September, the 11th Middlesex had commenced preparations for the general attack and trenches 81, 83 and 84 were ready with straw in the fire trench, while trench 82 had been supplied with 300 'Thelfallite' No. 1 Smoke Bombs. The Battalion's Battle Order can be summarized very briefly as 'light the straw and stay put' with point 17 of the Order stating in block capitals, 'NO ATTACK TO BE LAUNCHED WITHOUT DEFINITE ORDERS FROM HEADQUARTERS.' Another interesting extract from the Order tells us what was to happen should the trenches come under heavy enemy artillery fire. In this event 'only the officers, NCOs and Look-out men with their first relief in the fire trench are to remain at their posts. Similarly in the support trench. All remainder will be put in the slit trenches.'

Irrespective of the part the Battalion played in the early stages of the battle, Aby and his colleagues were stood-to early on the morning of the 25th. They wore full equipment minus packs, and they occupied trenches muddy from the previous day's rain. Elsewhere on the line, and perhaps in Aby's battalion too, men were to wear their gas-hoods with the lower edge (that was designed to be tucked into the collar) rolled up to their brows. Over these they were to have their caps placed on top and held in place by a length of string tied under the chin. A ridiculous sight but thought to be expedient. The gas-hoods in use at the time were of the PH (phenate-hexamine) type; basically a woollen hood soaked in a chemical and fitted with twin, round eye-lenses and a rubber exhalation tube. The wearer was meant to breathe in through the nose, with air passing in through the fabric, and breath out through the tube. In the event of a gas-attack they could be quickly rolled down and tucked in to give about fifteen minutes' protection. As can be imagined, they were stifling and gave any man exerting himself the feeling of being suffocated. Then the lenses would steam up making the wearer breathless and virtually blind.

The Germans were pioneers in the use of gas as a weapon and had used gas twice before, once on the Eastern and once on the Western Front. At the Battle of Loos the British were to use it for the first time, and with levels of success spanning the spectrum from fair to absolutely disastrous, according to varying wind directions along the line. Towards the northern limits of the initial attack, still some way south of Aby's position, Tommies were actually gassed by British releases of the chemical fog when the breeze blew it back into British trenches.

At 4.30 am heavy artillery, rifle and machine-gun fire was heard to the south, and half an hour later British artillery commenced a bombardment. The enemy replied by sending over the occasional whizz-bang. At 5.56 am the damp straw was ignited and the smoke curtain started. Aby must have wondered how long his luck would last out, for his section of the line was quiet although there was intensive artillery, rifle and machine-gun fire to both the north and the south. By 6.40 am the smoke curtain was still going well. The enemy were throwing over whizz-bangs and some high explosives were put into Battalion HQ at Houpline, but there was still hardly any rifle fire. A pre-dawn mist was alternately lifting and coming down, but the Battalion lookouts were able to determine that the enemy appeared to be sparse within their firing line and it was thought they were concentrated in their support lines.

By now, further to the south, closer to the small mining town of Loos, the battle proper was raging and thousands of men were dying. One tactic employed was to make rushes across no-mans land by platoon and there is record of one officer calling on his platoon, none of whom, except the sergeant, obeyed his command. He admonished them for cowards. His sergeant replied, 'Not cowards, Sir. Willing enough. But they're all fucking dead.'

For Aby and the 11th Middlesex, 7.30 am saw the smoke curtain virtually spent, and while battle continued to be joined in the south, it was eerily quiet. The Middlesex held the line according to the Battle Order and maintained a 'semblance of an impending attack'. The enemy started firing high explosives towards Houpline and Armentieres in the afternoon and drizzle set in that continued for most of the afternoon. The Middlesex opened rifle and machine-gun fire on enemy trenches and on roads to the enemy's rear, the German's replying with occasional shrapnel.

Things quietened down a little in the evening, with the Germans sending up a flare from their fire trench at 7.15 pm. From 10.00 pm onwards the 11th kept up steady rifle and machine-gun fire on enemy trenches, especially on the support trenches. The Germans fired back with machine-guns and several series of shots at short intervals. In the early hours of the 26th, the 11th mounted ten bombing patrols throwing between them about eighty bombs into enemy fire trenches. The only two parties of Germans seen were 'successfully bombed'.

For all this artillery, rifle and machine-gun fire, it seems almost miraculous that Aby's battalion suffered only one casualty, and that only a slight wound that did not take the man from his duty. Further south on the line, tens of thousands of British and Commonwealth troops had lost their lives. It seemed that the Ace of Spades – the 'death-card' – was looking after its own and that the 11th came under a protective charm. At 7.00 pm on 26 September 1915, the 11th Middlesex were relieved in the trenches by the 6th Battalion Durham Light Infantry, and exhausted but mercifully spared, the Middlesex men made their way to billets near Armentieres station.

The 11th Middlesex received orders to proceed to the Lillers-Chocques area in preparation for them to join the battle proper. Following news that other New Army regiments had distinguished themselves in the battle, the 12th Division were reported to be keen for the opportunity to do the same and they left their old area, filled with a mixture of anticipation and trepidation. 'Some took their departure by train, some by bus and some by road, but all went singing and in the highest spirit.'

The 11th were one of the battalions that 'took their departure' by train, but first they had to get to the station. They set off at 7.00 am on 28 September to march the route and were all aboard and ready for departure by 9.00 am. They arrived at Chocques (three kilometres west-north-west of Bethune) at 11.30 am and then set off on another march. Their ordered destination was 'the town' of La Vallee, three kilometres to the north – although a good deal further by road due to the indirect route. They arrived only to find that 'the town' was in fact only a single farm and far too small to billet an entire battalion. Staff arrangements had fallen below requirements yet again. In fact, Staff Officers were most noticeable by their absence, and the Battalion had to send out its own billeting parties in order to secure shelter in the farms to the north-west of Gonnehem.

Although settled in their self-arranged billets by half past four, the frustration of the tired men was to continue as Transport did not arrive until 9.30 pm, no arrangements having been made by Staff 'to inform Transport where Battalion was or to inform Battalion where transport was'.

Next morning, Wednesday, 29 September, the 11th Middlesex joined the other battalions with which they were brigaded, and at 10.00 am set off on a ten kilometre route march to Verquigneul, a small town on the other side of Bethune. From here they would make final preparations before rejoining battle. They found the route to be very busy with troop movements to and from the front. Seeing the companies of tired, wounded men leaving the front must have had a sobering effect. They arrived to find that Staff had made billeting arrangements for only 230 men. Again the Battalion had to rely on its own resources, finally settling the men by 6.30 pm. It was on this day that Lieutenant Colonel Ingle returned from sick leave and resumed command from Major Newton.

At 10.00 am on the following day, Ingle and Captain Pargiter inspected the trenches in the vicinity of 'the lone tree' (a landmark roughly equidistant between the village of Loos and the Hohenzollern Redoubt) in preparation for the Battalion to take the line. This they did later in the afternoon, marching from their billets via the shattered town of Vermelles to trenches, which had recently been those of the enemy.

George Coppard notes:

Next day we slogged it to Vermelles, a war-scarred little town in the coal-mining area close to the scene of the battle. The struggle which had begun five days before our arrival was working up to a full cry. Salvoes of coal-boxes were crashing down nearby at the foot of the Vermelles-Hulloch road. Our artillery – the howitzers at our backs and the field guns on both sides of us – was firing flat out. Its deafening thunder threatened our ear drums. It was inspiring, though uncomfortable, for soon eighteen-pounder shells were screaming just over our heads, an experience to which we were not yet accustomed.

The 11th Middlesex relieved the 2nd Coldstream Guards completing the relief at 1.00 am the next morning in very wet weather. There were no Middlesex casualties despite incessant shelling on both sides.

Official accounts tell us that 35 and 36 Brigades were next to each other in the line. It may be further deduced from a comparison of George Coppard's account and the 11th Middlesex War Diary, that although in different brigades, George and Aby were at this time in the same part of the front; that is, close to the Vermelles-Hulloch Road. So when George describes the scene we may be certain that it was the same as that witnessed by Aby.

> And there, stretching for several hundred yards on the right of the road, lay masses of British dead, struck down by machine-gun and rifle fire. Shells from enemy field batteries had been pitching into these bodies, flinging them into dreadful postures. As they mostly belonged to Highland regiments there was a fantastic display of colour from their kilts, glengarries and bonnets, and also from the bloody wounds on their bare limbs. The warm weather had darkened their faces and, shrouded as they were with the sickly odour of death, it was repulsive to be near them.

At this time, the twin-towered steel pithead structure at Loos was still standing, although after several days bombardment this unmistakable landmark that the Tommies called 'Tower Bridge' would fall as another casualty of battle.

This, their twelfth stretch in the trenches, was to be the busiest so far for Aby and the men of the 11th Middlesex. The tour was to last for seven days during which time the men were to be subjected to the heaviest bombardments of artillery shells they had yet experienced. Battalion HQ, now sited in the old German fire trench, was to narrowly escape destruction and parties of men numbering in the hundreds had to dig new trenches in front of the British line and later, new communications trenches. At the end of the tour five more Middlesex men had lost their lives and seventeen were wounded, but given the intensity and duration of the bombardments, this is little short of a miracle.

The tour was not entirely without respite for there was an occasional 'comparatively quiet' morning or afternoon, but taken as a whole, the line took a battering. One quiet morning though, that of Wednesday, 6 October, prompted speculation that the coal box gun of the enemy had been 'put out of action' or was at least 'taking a rest'. Maybe it was merely gloating, because four days earlier the divisional commander and his ADC (Captain C.C. Towers, DSO), were killed when a coal box blew them up in trenches near the Hulloch Road.

Major General Wing, a former gentleman of artillery himself, had been keen to inspect the position of a battery near the front. Shell fire was incessant, and the British gunners were hard pressed to find field gun positions free from German observers. Wing hoped that his experience would furnish a solution, but a shell exploded just in front of him and he was killed instantly. He was the third officer of general rank to lose his life in the Battle of Loos.

In one of his letters home, Aby perhaps gives a clue that Wing was well thought of by his men. Aby writes in January 1916:

I am sending this photo of one of the officers who was killed ...
He was very good to us ... Please frame it for a keepsake.

Aby does not name the officer, or if he did his name is in part of the letter that has been edited out, but it is most likely to be Wing. At the time Aby wrote, only three officers of the 11th Middlesex had been killed; a captain and two lieutenants. The deaths of none of these young officers are likely to have engendered the production of photos for the men, even if they were known for their kindness. It is difficult to see how an enlisted man could obtain a photo of an officer, unless it be that of a high ranking one whose death resulted in the circulation of postcards to those formerly under his command, as mementos.

By 6.30 pm on 7 October, Aby's battalion had been relieved in the trenches by the 2nd Black Watch. Exhausted and dirty from the wet, muddy trenches, and with nerves frayed from the most intense bombardment they had yet endured, the men would have been hardly recognizable from the comparatively fresh battalion that took over the line seven days earlier.

On the move newly-come units were easy to tell from those that have been out some months. The older lot crawl, the new march; the old plod along, mostly quietly and seriously, the new sing and whistle, and cock an eye at any responsive woman.

At least there were billets to look forward to and a chance to get away from the mud for a few days. Think again Aby! Having been told there were billets waiting for them, the Middlesex men were instead bivouacked in a swampy wood that formed part of the grounds of the Chateau de Vaudricourt. They arrived at 1.30 am and settled down as best they could.

Aby was part of the lucky majority who only had to endure the unsuitable conditions until 4.00 pm on Saturday, 9 October. He was with those who were found billets at Verquin. Both A Company and Transport had to stay in the wood. We do not know if Aby's luck held out, but he may have been among roughly one-third of the Battalion that was able to bathe at a mine just south of Verquin. Eighty men from each company partook of the facility on the Tuesday, ironically the same day they later rejoined the muddy trenches.

What were these baths like? As with billets and food and any other supposed comfort we may think of, the short answer is to say they were variable. As we have seen, sometimes the men simply bathed in rivers, although this practice became increasingly unsuitable as the colder weather drew in. Sometimes the Engineers and Sanitary companies set up Heath Robinson-like contraptions to give the men a shower. Sometimes there was even hot water. Frederic Manning was an author who served as a private soldier in a section of the front close to the part of the line Aby knew. In his novel *Her Privates We*, he writes about bathing in such detailed terms we must conclude they are based largely, if not completely, on his own real-life experiences. He speaks of the men marching by company to the baths.

They stripped to the buff in one room, handed over towel, socks, shirt and underpants to the men in charge, who gave them clean things in exchange: these were rolled up in a bundle, ready, and a man took what he was given without question, except in the case of an impossible misfit or a garment utterly useless, in which case he might ask his sergeant-major to intervene, though even his intervention was not always effective.

95

Having experienced all this as an enlisted man, Manning was in a good position to comment on the petty injustices that were the constant lot of Tommy.

It was invariably the same at casualty-clearing-stations or divisional baths, the lead-swingers in charge and their chums took the best of the stuff they handled, and the fighting men had to make shift as best they could with their leavings. The men left their clean change with their boots and khaki, and passed naked into one large room in which casks, sawn in two and standing in rows, did duty for baths. There were a few improvised showers. Here they splashed and soaped themselves, with a riotous noisiness and a good deal of indecent horseplay.

Manning goes on to detail the plight of the young and shy soldier.

'Dost turn thysen to t' wall, lad, so's us 'uns sha'n't see tha dick?' one man shouted at a shy young newcomer; and when the boy turned a red and indignant face over his shoulder, he was met with derision, and another man pulled him out of the tub, and wrestled with him, slippery as they both were with soap. They were distinctly fresh. Rude and brutal as it was, there was a boisterous good-humour about it, and laughing at his show of temper and humiliation, some other men intervened, and they let him slip out of their hands and back to his tub, where he continued the washing of himself as modestly as he could.

After drying and dressing, the men marched away for another company to take its place. In the case of the 11th Middlesex on 12 October 1915, they marched from their bath to start another tour in the trenches. This time they took up positions in the ruined houses and trenches to the south side of Vermelles, and prepared to play their part in the next stage of the battle.

The objectives of the 12th Division were the Gun Trench and the Quarries; the assault scheduled to begin at 2.00 pm on Wednesday, 13 October following a two-hour artillery bombardment of enemy lines and the formation of a smokescreen. Each man was to carry equipment including his greatcoat, a waterproof sheet, a full waterbottle, his gas helmet ready for use and a pair of goggles worn at the peak of his cap in case the enemy used tear gas. He was also to carry sandbags, and 250 rounds of ammunition – one hundred more than usual. Some of the men were to be equipped with wire cutters, periscopes and entrenching tools.

The plan was for the artillery to commence bombardment at noon, and then to cease-fire at three minutes to one. At 1.00 pm they were to begin a short period of rapid-fire, then to continue as before until 2.00 pm. The reasoning was that the Germans would consider the bombardment complete when the guns ceased just before one, and man their firing line in anticipation of an attack, only to be caught out by the ensuing rapid artillery fire. It was further hoped that at 2.00 pm, having been once bloodied, they would be twice shy and remain under cover, giving the true attack a head start. In the event, the Germans proved to be not nearly so gullible.

As soon as the British bombardment began, the Germans retaliated with an equally ferocious and damaging counter-bombardment. Damage was severe on the British side, though casualties light. Then at 2.00 pm, the smokescreen lifted far more quickly than anticipated, exposing the advancing British to German observation. The Germans stood-to and were ready for the fight.

With 35 Brigade attacking on the left (the Quarries) and 37 Brigade on the right (Gun Trench), 36 Brigade had to hold position and stand ready. Lieutenant Leach and fifty bombers of D Company were sent to the left to support the troops of 35 Brigade, and although they were sorely needed, they did not return to the Battalion for almost two days despite requests, by which time they were exhausted from constant bombing. At one stage they held part of the line 'practically by themselves'.

As part of 36 Brigade's relief of 37 Brigade, the 11th took over the front trenches from the 6th Royal West Kents and the 7th East Surreys on 14 October.

Staff arrangements for relief very poor – we were not told which units we were relieving and had to find our own ration dump during night. No arrangements for water.

The Germans continued to be very active and laid down a heavy barrage of high explosive shells and aerial torpedoes on the front line.

This is another sentence quickly written and quickly read, that is only too easily passed over. Pause for just a while and try to empathize with the men who had to endure hours, where each moment was crowded with enough mayhem to fill an age.

In two places the parapet was entirely blasted away for a stretch of fifty yards. Seven men died and eight were wounded, including No. 179 Private Stanley Jones, a stretcher-bearer who was noted for being 'always on the spot when required'. Ironically, he was wounded while bearing an injured German from the front line to the dressing station. Again the next day, the trenches were shelled and once again the parapets levelled. The bombing continued day and night. An officer – Second Lieutenant Brodie – was wounded together with eleven enlisted men and a further six men were killed.

One man – Private Lloyd – had fallen wounded in front of the parapet. CSM Charles Bentley, who had frequently exposed himself to enemy rifle and machine-gun fire in broad daylight so that he could bandage the wounded and get them to safety, once again leapt to the aid of the injured man. No. 983 Private James Howe assisted him. They were sitting ducks, and CSM Bentley's luck ran out when he was shot through the heart. Howe continued to work on Lloyd under heavy fire, and managed to get him safely away to a dressing station.

On the 17th, shelling was so intense that for the third time in a row the parapet was levelled and all the work of building it up overnight was undone. And for the third day in a row, lives were lost (four) and men were wounded (ten). One of the wounded on this occasion was No. 268 Sergeant Thomas Moorhouse who was noted for his 'extraordinary good reconnaissance, patrol and bombing work' and was always said to show great coolness and self-reliance. That night men from C and D Companies helped men of the 8th Royal Fusiliers to build up the parapets once more.

Monday, 18 October proved to be the Battalion's worst day for casualties so far (and Aby would not live to see another quite so bad), with the Germans continuing their barrage, once again levelling the parapets and raining down heavy fire on the trenches all day long. Especial attention was paid to those occupied by A and C Companies. Many men were buried when high explosive shells caused parts of the trench system to collapse, and many others suffered from concussion. To make matters worse, some British shells were bursting early, right over the Middlesex men and this continued during the day and night. Captain H.G. Money, the only officer hurt, was actually caught by a short bursting British shell. Captain Harold Peploe won praise for steadying the men who were under particularly intense fire from high explosive shells and aerial torpedoes. Fifteen men were killed and thirty-five wounded, and Peploe himself was wounded during the bombardment.

And still the shelling continued. Another man was killed on the 19th; one officer and fourteen men were wounded. At 4.00 pm the 11th Argyle & Sutherland Highlanders began relieving the 11th Middlesex, but an hour and a half into the relief operation, the Germans attacked positions to the right and increased their shelling of the Middlesex trenches, also opening up with heavy rifle and machine-gun fire. The Germans were repulsed, with British losses, and the fighting subsided at 7.30 pm.

The relief was completed in the early hours of the 20th, but this was not a true relief in the usual sense. The Middlesex men simply exchanged one section of the line for another. It was only D Company though, who took over a fire trench; one that had recently been a German one. Aby in B Company, together with A and C Companies went into the reserve trench that had been the British fire trench until ground was gained in battle. Second Lieutenant Leach and the Battalion bombers were fitted out with a full supply of new bombs and went in support of D Company. It was during the night of the 20th/21st that the bombers followed Leach's quick thinking commands and turned a close disaster into victory.

Leach effected a counter-attack on an advancing force of Germans who had caused men of the 9th Royal Sussex to run for it. The incident is best described in the actual words of the report written to Lieutenant Colonel Ingle.

I was just writing to you when yours arrived.

My second in command Major Copemen who was in command of my Companies reports as follows:-

'On the night of 20th–21st October there was an alarm at the bombing post of the new trench and urgent calls for re-enforcement's. I proceeded there and found the bombing party who were on duty at the time viz: 7th Royal Sussex had been surprised and lost their heads and temporarily quitted the barricade. They had suffered heavy casualties and the officer's nerves were shaken.'

One wonders, had the ranking officer been an enlisted man, would he have faced charges of a kind that carried the death penalty?

> 'On the arrival of Lieut Leach and the Middlesex Bombers this officer took charge and quickly bombed the enemy beyond the barricade and restored the situation.
>
> The behaviour and throwing of the Middlesex Bombers was splendid and Lieut Leach should submit his own names.'
>
> I am awfully glad to be able to report so well and most grateful to you and the Middlesex Regiment for their help.

The report was dated 21/10/15 and signed by Lieutenant Colonel G.C. Lewis, DSO, Commanding Officer of the 9th Essex Regiment. Lieutenant Leach was awarded the Military Cross for his promptness, bravery and initiative. Three of his bombers – No. 11098 Lance Corporal Cecil Smart, No. 5767 Private Alfred Brown and No. 495 Private Herbert Havers – won Distinguished Conduct Medals for 'dash and disregard of danger, and for effective bomb throwing driving the enemy out of the trench'. The awards were promulgated on 15 December.

The busiest and bloodiest tour for the Middlesex men so far, ended with relief by the 10th Scottish Rifles at 4.30 pm on Thursday, 21 October 1915. Since arriving in France, the Battalion had now lost sixty-seven men killed – not including those men who were initially wounded and later died of wounds – and 138 wounded. That represents a statistic of close to one in five men of the Battalion strength either killed or wounded.

The relief of the 11th Middlesex was excruciatingly slow as the trenches were hopelessly blocked due to a breakdown in trench movement protocols. The 9th Essex Regiment were using the incoming trenches to get out, which led to the relieving units being unable to take up their posts as expeditiously as they otherwise could. It meant that after eight days, the Middlesex men were held up for another two hours. It is no wonder they left the trenches exhausted, battered and with morale worn thin. Even taking away the bombardments they had endured, the trenches were muddy and wet and the nights were bitter. Neither trench waders or winter gear had been issued.

Desperate for rest, Staff again let the men of the 11th down. Having been promised motor buses from Noyelles-les-Vermelles to their billets, the Middlesex arrived at the town at 9.00 pm to find only twenty-five buses had been laid on – not just for the Battalion, but for the whole Brigade. Aby had a good soaking, having to wait with the rest of the 11th from 9.00 pm until 2.30 am in the pouring rain before they could leave. By this time the men had not eaten for eighteen hours.

And still the nightmare was not over. When the Middlesex men eventually arrived at their allotted billets in the early hours of the morning, they found one of them to be occupied by a signal company and another by a platoon of the 9th Royal Fusiliers. Lieutenant Colonel Ingle blew his top and personally threw them out. The men were finally settled in their Fouquieres billets at 5.00 am and 'rested all day'.

Again, 'rest' did not quite mean all it implied. On this occasion it certainly meant freedom from manning up working parties. But equally as certain was that filthy, mud-encrusted uniforms and soggy boots had to be ameliorated and returned to parade ground perfection (or at least as close as was possible), for on the next day the 11th were to be inspected by the new general officer commanding the Ace of Spades Division. They worked hard on their uniforms, but no arrangements had been made for the men to bathe.

Major General Arthur B. Scott, DSO (later Sir Arthur B. Scott, KCB) took command of the 12th Division shortly after the death of Major General Wing. He would retain command until April 1918, and was the Divisional Commander for the rest of Aby's life, making some adverse comment on Aby's court martial papers as we shall see later. He inspected the 11th Middlesex on 23 October and addressed the troops, saying that he was very pleased with their work in general, and especially impressed with the work of the bombers under Lieutenant Leach.

The 11th Middlesex men had certainly earned a rest, and at last they got one. The Battle of Loos had petered out and the men had been through their first important engagement. Yes, of course, there were drills and classes (machine-gun, signalling and general attack), and yes, some of these classes were carried out in muddy trenches (to the rear) in pouring rain. But the Middlesex men were out of the active trenches and any amount of training, no matter how uncomfortable, was preferable to the battering they had recently survived.

On Tuesday, 26 October, the Battalion marched six kilometres from Fouquieres to new billets at Sailly Labourse. Classes continued and there was a very welcome relief from the need to fill working parties. The Battalion also made an arrangement with the officer commanding the Sanitary Company of the Guards Division, and thus secured for their use a bathing facility at a mine in the small town of Annequin, just to the west of Sailly Labourse. At last the men were able to have a bath, but if George Coppard's experience held the same for the Middlesex men, they were to end up with black behinds from sitting on benches covered with coal-dust while they dried themselves. In Coppard's case, a cause for much hilarity.

On the 28th, the officers went to see the new trenches. The attack was practised morning and afternoon of 31 October and one man was injured during bomb practice.

The next day, the attack was again practised in the morning, and in the afternoon it was time to return to the trenches for another active tour – their fourteenth in all since arriving in France. The evidence suggests that Aby was not one to volunteer to participate in operations, so it is unlikely that he was a bomber. Bombers tended to be volunteers and were often required for patrols in advance of the firing line. But neither was he a 'skrimshanker' or shirker, for there was no room in the Army to disobey orders, and a man ordered to take part in a patrol either went or faced serious charges. There is no evidence whatsoever to suggest that Aby had anything but a clean sheet as far as discipline is concerned. Rather, he was one of the majority who did what was required of him and hoped for as quiet a time as the War would allow.

At 1.00 pm on Monday, 1 November 1915, nine days after their last tour, the 11th Middlesex relieved the 6th Royal West Kents in trenches west of the Hohenzollern Redoubt. Aby was posted with the rest of B Company to man the trenches known as Sticky Trench and the Hog's Back. The relief was carried out in steady rain which persisted all day and all through the night. They had not inherited decent trenches, as the War Diary entry for 2 November clearly shows.

Continuous rain all day and night. Parapets kept falling in at 10 & 20 yard stretches. Impossible to repair with sandbags. No revetting material sent though urgently applied for. No dug-outs or shelter of any sort, so men have to remain on fire-step day and night. Impossible for them to lie down as mud too deep. No sleep possible from cold & wet.

And then of course there was enemy shelling. Conditions did not improve, and inevitably a serious toll was taken on the men's health. The morale and health of the Battalion were beginning to show signs of breaking down. For the first time, the War Diary begins to list the numbers of men made ineffective as a direct cause of the wet and the lack of sleep. The men spent a lot of time cleaning out the trenches and rebuilding the parapets with the standard equipment available to them, only to find out later that eighteen 'mud scoops' had been allocated to the Battalion. These had been lying idle at a Royal Engineers dump half a mile from Battalion HQ. Nobody had informed the Middlesex men, and as they were seen to be out of use, Staff then rubbed salt into the wound by complaining that the 11th were doing no work.

Staff further endeared themselves to the 11th Middlesex on 5 November when Major J.K. Cochrane of General Staff visited a Middlesex trench. Restrained exasperation can be felt rising from between the lines of the War Diary's entry for that day.

An officer from 12th Div Staff went round one trench & said of course things were bad but that they weren't anything like what had been reported by us. All ranks had now [been] soaked though & standing continuously in mud & water for over 100 hours with no chance of sleep or even lying down.

Aby and his company had been at the brunt of enemy shelling that day. All its officers had been wounded, and all but one made ineffective by their wounds. Only Second Lieutenant Lewis was able to stay with B Company, and he himself was badly shaken by a shell which also wounded Second Lieutenants McDonald and MacIlwaine. Casualties include a list of those sick for the second time.

63 sick as follow:- frozen feet 40, rheumatism 9, influenza and bronchitis 8, various 6.

The previous day's casualties had included the following.

78 other ranks sick as follows:- Rheumatism, cold & chill 25, exhaustion 28, frozen feet (mostly men who were out here last winter) 18, shock from H.E. 7.

The Middlesex men spent the rest of the tour working daily to repair trenches, putting up with the awful conditions and surviving heavy bombardment from the Germans. Even their relief by the 7th Royal Sussex Regiment was delayed by three hours 'owing to heavy shelling of all trenches & HQ by enemy'. They then took over the reserve trenches evacuated by their relief battalion, and set to work cleaning and building them up.

These experiences over the last tour and rest period were very much the pattern throughout November and into December, although there may have been a little relief for Aby and the other Jewish lads from the 7th, 12th and 47th Divisions. The Senior Jewish Chaplain, the Rev. Michael Adler, arranged for a celebration of the Jewish festival of Chanukkah. Held a little earlier than usual, the participants gathered in the theatre at Lillers, and maybe Aby was one of the hundred-strong congregation. His battalion was not in the trenches at that time and his billet was not far from Lillers, so depending on the permission of his officer, he would have had the opportunity to attend. Festival candles were lit and after the service, the lads gathered at a local *estaminet* for a tea party organized by RSM Harris of the 4th London Regiment. One of the soldiers suggested that a collection be made on behalf of the distressed Jews in Poland, and £3 was raised.

Back to the daily grind, and working parties were very much on the menu, as were several changes of billets. Training was also maintained, with the occasional route march thrown in. An entry in the War Diary gives a good indication that Captain Pargiter was thoroughly fed up with the whole situation. He writes of the last part of a large working party's return to the Battalion.

10/12/15
4 pm. 1 officer & 80 men of working party returned, soaked through and tired out. They had to march out from Bethune though Bde. had promised to send them in lorries. Result of this working party having to be found by us – 1/3 of battalion tired out and soaked through for 36 hours, before Battalion goes into front line trenches.

The next day saw an entirely unexpected and unannounced draft of 132 other ranks marching in to join the 11th, mostly from the 1st and 3rd Battalions of the Middlesex Regiment. All ranks had their feet rubbed with whale oil before they relieved the 2nd Argyle & Sutherland Highlanders. They went by way of a boot drying room near Festubert where gumboots were issued. The theme of this tour was pumping out flooded trenches, being shelled and gaining some success in sniping at the enemy, whose trenches were, by such observations as were possible, just as bad as the British ones.

On Thursday, 16 December the men got a new issue of uniform. From what we have learnt of their experiences, one wonders if their old 'khaki' served any purpose whatsoever as clothing. They must have been little more than tattered, mud-stiffened, louse-infested rags.

The 19th December saw the 11th taking up billets in a former tobacco factory in Bethune, and the men probably thought they had fallen on their feet for once. The accommodation was spacious and dry, with plenty of room to carry out the necessities of army life. Aby was more than likely reminded of his sister Kate, for instead of becoming a buttonhole maker like many a tailor's daughter, she found employment in the cigarette making industry. However, they did not have long to enjoy their comparative comfort on that first day. They moved into the billet at 9.00 am and by 4.30 pm the whole Battalion was required for a carrying fatigue. They came back from the working party at 4.00 am.

A week later, the 11th Middlesex relieved the 5th Berkshire Regiment in trenches north of Givenchy. It was a slow process, beginning at 11.30 am and not complete until 7.00 pm. The conditions here were even worse than those previous had been.

If the last front was bad, this one beggared description.

The History of the 12th (Eastern) Division in the Great War, 1914–1918 continues.

In the Festubert section, the country, principally water meadows, was intensely wet and water-logged, the rain had filled the trenches, and pumping had not overcome this trouble. Along a large proportion of the front line the parapet appeared in the form of islands above the water.

Aby's company was posted to three areas of trench, called Princes Street, George Street and Le Plantain. Conditions in Princes Street were so bad that all eighteen men posted there had to gather on an

105

island, as the rest of the trench was untenable. The enemy was quiet, but the rain continued.

So bad were the conditions that drying rooms and soup-kitchens were set up close to the front, the latter dispensing up to 1,500 bowls of soup a day to the 12th Division men at the front.

Early on the morning of Christmas Eve, the Germans blew up a mine to the right of the Middlesex positions and laid down a fierce barrage of all trenches for a few minutes. Later in the day the Germans made two attacks but were beaten back by the actions of the Middlesex bombers.

During the afternoon No. 803 Private Worrall was engaged in bombing, but due to his hands being slick with mud, he dropped a bomb in the trench. He immediately shouted a warning to his fellows and proceeded to stomp the bomb as deep into the mud as he could. It only had a five-second fuse and it exploded, wounding him in the leg, but his quick actions meant that no others were hurt.

Then came Christmas Day 1915, and there was to be no repeat of the unofficial ceasefires that bloomed at many places all along the front a year earlier. The men were in no mood for truces and harboured only ill will for their enemies, or more accurately, all good will had been blasted from them. The General Staff had issued severe warnings that there was to be no fraternization, but the warnings were not needed.

> Bombers were lively in the early morning giving the enemy Xmas greetings with 48 bombs. Only two were sent in reply. During early morning enemy shelled our trenches heavily doing a good deal of damage to Poppy Redoubt & New Cut. In the afternoon he shelled Le Plantain. Our guns retaliated and stopped his firing.

Good will was not extended to all men this Christmastide, but at least the Middlesex men completed another tour and were relieved by their old friends of the 9th Royal Fusiliers, getting to their billets at Le Quesnoy at 10.00 pm. But it was only a quick respite, for they were back in the trenches on 27 December. It was a quiet night, but next day there was some shelling, and on Wednesday, 29 December 1915 at five-past-seven in the morning the Germans exploded a mine. It created a huge crater which they then tried to occupy. They failed and were beaten back.

It was during their attack that the Germans made use of weapons new to the 12th Division men – although used on a previous occasion against the 11th Middlesex. They were mechanical bomb-throwers, or catapults. Two Middlesex men were killed, and five, including Aby, were wounded. The exact details of his injuries are lost to history, but it is known he was hurt in the back and suffered shock. The most likely cause of his wound was a piece of shrapnel or other matter flung out from the explosion of the mine.

Aby's parents and his sister Kate learnt of his wounding on receipt of a yellow form from the Infantry Records Office at Hounslow.

15/1/1916
Sir,
    I regret to inform you that a report has this day been received from the War Office to the effect that Private Abraham Harris, Regt. 11th Battn. Middlesex G.S. is ill at 38th Field Ambulance, France, suffering from wounds and shock (mine explosion).

Sylvia Pankhurst reported that the family also received a letter from the wife of Aby's commanding officer saying that Aby was wounded and it was too early to say whether he would stay in France or be sent to a hospital in England. Although unlikely, it is possible that Mrs Ingle wrote to Mr and Mrs Bevistein, but it is more probable that the letter was from Aby's platoon or company commander's wife, or perhaps even from the wife of an officer with the Field Ambulance. The actual document is lost, and Pankhurst did not include a name in her publication, so we can never know. The reference does perhaps indicate that Aby's wound was a little more than superficial. Certainly, the Bevisteins were terrified by the news and eagerly awaited a letter from Aby himself.

What pains or fears Aby suffered we do no know. Having lived with death and the fear of death or injury for so long, the fact that he had incurred the latter may have even come as some relief. Men were often cheerful, despite pain, after receiving a wound, convinced that they had 'copped a blighty one'.

Chapter 10

Respite and Flight

Oh, that I had wings like a dove: for then
I would flee away, and be at rest.

Prayer Book, 1662

There are no records to tell us whether Aby was patched up at a dressing station in the trenches, whether he was a stretcher case or if he made his way to the Field Ambulance under his own steam, but there is evidence that he had to spend nine days in bed. Given this degree of immobility the likelihood is that he was taken out of the trenches, either carried or on a stretcher. He was treated at the 38th Field Ambulance for some time, and maybe even for his entire 'hospital' stay, although that would have been unusual. A Field Ambulance, which was in fact a medical facility not too far away from the front and not a vehicle as the name suggests, was not designed for long-stay patients.

Each division had three Field Ambulances, and for the 12th Division these were the 36th, 37th and 38th. A more modern equivalent would be the US Mobile Army Surgical Hospitals, made famous by the TV comedy-drama *MASH*. Each had an establishment of ten officers and 224 men who were divided into two sections and those sections were themselves further divided into stretcher-bearer and tented subsections. At the time of Aby's admittance, Lieutenant Colonel G.H. Goddard, DSO, commanded the 38th Field Ambulance. A Field Ambulance's capacity for casualties was 150, though this number was often far exceeded in the height of battle.

The letter from the unknown officer's wife suggests that there was some uncertainty as to Aby's case, and it is therefore possible that he was, at some stage, transferred to one of the Casualty Clearing Stations (CCSs). These were more substantial affairs and located further from the front in areas of relative safety, but they were still sufficiently mobile to be packed up and moved on as need arose. As the name implies, CCSs were set up to determine the course of action to be taken with the wounded men, and to ensure that they were sent in the right direction. They could be sent to a proper hospital well behind the lines, returned to duty after a short stay or even shipped out to Blighty – every man's dearest wish. In the event, if Aby did get as far as a CCS, he got no further.

Aby wrote many letters home while he was ill, the first pre-dating the Army notice by more than a fortnight and quite possibly reaching Anthony Street well in advance of anything official. Dated 1 January 1916, apart from indications that Aby was a little frustrated with the postal arrangements, he seems primarily concerned with putting his mother's mind at ease.

Dear Mother,
   I am very sorry I did not write before now, but we were in the trenches on Christmas Day and we had a lot to do. Also I was taken ill and I was sent to the hospital. I am feeling a little better, so don't get upset; also don't send any letters to the company, because I won't get them. Also you cannot send any letters to the hospital, as I won't get them. Dear Mother, do not worry, I will be all right. Hoping all of you are getting on well. I was only hurt in the back. I will try to send you letters every few days if I can to let you know how I am getting on. We get plenty of food in the hospital. Dear Mother, I know it will break your heart this, but don't get upset about it. I will be all right, but would very much like to see you, but I will try my best.

The two pieces of evidence that suggest Aby stayed at the Field Ambulance are the official notification from the War Office and the next letter from Aby.

6th January 1916
I have been in hospital for nine days, lying in bed all the time and now I have a sore heel ... I had it cut today and it is getting better.

'Nine days' takes Aby back to the day he was wounded. He mentions lying in bed all the time, and makes no reference to a transfer. There were other letters, but their content has not been noted. The next letter that there is any reference to was dated 20 January 1916, and was written from a farm in the tiny village of La Flandrie situated three kilometres north of Lillers, a town famous to the Tommies for its cakes and fancy pastries.

Dear Mother,
    I am quite well, and I came out of hospital on Wednesday (19th).

One wonders just how well Aby really was. From his next letter, it would appear that something was playing on his mind. Perhaps he had received a letter from home, and some reference or other to his recent injury and illness puzzled him. On the 24th he wrote:

Dear Mother,
    You don't know how I was longing for a letter from you! I would like to know what the War Office said was the matter with me.

While Aby was in hospital, he had missed one uncomfortable but uneventful tour of the trenches during which one man had been wounded. Following that, the 11th Middlesex had been out on rest doing a tour of the billets around Festubert, Le Touret and Les Chocquaux. He had also missed out on a number of typical rest-day working parties, and Christmas dinner, which his colleagues enjoyed in their Les Choquaux billets on 2 January.

Three days before Aby's release, the Middlesex men had moved to billets in and between the settlements of Le Cornet Bourdois and La Flandrie, half a kilometre to the south. Aby was billeted into a farmhouse belonging to Madame Cordionne, situated on the north side of the road that ran between the railway lines and the town of Busnes. Typical of the farmhouses of the area, it comprised a building set about a small central courtyard, the external walls continuous and windowless so giving the impression of defensibility and a design similar to a Roman villa, albeit on a much less grand scale.

Aby returned to his comrades at a time of spit and polish in preparation for a brigade inspection the following day. There was ceremonial drill to practise and one wonders how Aby's newly lanced foot held out. On Thursday, 20 January 1916, Brigadier General Boyd-Moss paraded his brigade (made up of the 8th and 9th Battalions Royal Fusiliers, the 7th Royal Sussex and the 11th Middlesex) for inspection by General Joseph-Jacques-Cesaire Joffre, Commander of the French armies.

The next few days were spent training and attending classes. In his free time, Aby may well have joined other Middlesex men on a trip down to 'the rather grubby little town' of Lillers, sampling some of the cakes available there or visiting an *estaminet*. This period really was a rest without working parties, and there were only daily inspections, drill and standard fatigues to carry out in addition to the training. Even the fourteen-mile route march the Middlesex men accomplished on Tuesday, 25 January was little compared to their recent experiences. Part of the Battalion was inspected by Brigadier General Boyd-Moss on the Wednesday, and the officers either enjoyed or endured RSO (Riding School for Officers) depending on their affinity with horses. It was also on Wednesday when the 11th Middlesex lost its Regimental Sergeant Major. Far from being killed, RSM Foster's warrant was replaced with a commission, and he was appointed to the 13th East Surrey Regiment as Quartermaster with the rank of full lieutenant.

Sitting in Madame Cordionne's farmhouse, Aby wrote to his mother about a deceased officer who had been 'very good to us' and enclosed a photo of the man as a keepsake.

The days passed with various officers being posted to training or to the machine-gun company and there was another route march – part of divisional manoeuvres – on 30th January when the Middlesex men were marched to the village of Estree Blanche where they had to wait for four hours for billets. On the next day, they marched back to Le Cornet Bourdois and their old billets.

The period out of the trenches stretched into another week and the 12th Division men must have begun to feel like human beings again, but Aby's recent close encounter with death must have been playing on his mind. The intensity of manoeuvres and preparations could only mean that something big was being planned. A successful soldier lives for the moment, and enjoys his comforts while they can be had. It does no good to dwell on tomorrow. But Aby and many of his comrades were not natural soldiers, nor were they in any way cut out for that kind of life. Knowing what life at the front was like after his

111

seven months of fighting, and realizing that the same was to come again, Aby must have felt the weight of the future approaching like an implacable doom. Sometimes anticipation of an event is far more stressful than the event itself. There is time for the mind to ponder and to plumb the dark depths of fear and imagination. For men who had witnessed death at close hand, who had marched to the front past fields deep with dead and mutilated soldiers, the imminent probability of more of the same must have been almost impossible to bear.

The effect of anticipation on morale was not entirely lost on the officer class, and efforts were made to distract the men. A divisional football tournament was arranged and by all accounts was greatly enjoyed by the men, with the 11th Middlesex's old partners in the Trench-Relief-Two-step – the 9th Royal Fusiliers – winning the final. Then there was the Army Service Corps' Captain Bayard who took over the Bethune Theatre and put on a production of Aladdin.

Aby left the farmhouse at La Flandrie on Saturday, 5 February 1916 when the Battalion marched five kilometres to billets at Gonnehem, the little town they had stayed at just before the 12th Division's main contribution to the Battle of Loos. Training continued, and two days later, at 4.30 pm on 7 February, Major General Scott again inspected the Battalion. He presented Private Alfred Brown with the Distinguished Conduct Medal ribbon for his actions of 20/21 October. On 10 February the 11th Battalion officers went to visit the trenches their men would soon take over. It was also on the 10th that Michael Adler, the Chaplain nicknamed (by himself) the wandering Jew, visited some units of the 12th Division.

The next day Aby was on the move again, marching back towards the front. The destination of the Middlesex men was Sailly Labourse, and the direct route was fourteen kilometres straight through Bethune. It was a wet day, and the men – and heaven forbid, the officers – were soon soaked through. On past Staff performance, the Battalion was probably not at all surprised that billeting arrangements were poor. Billets were eventually found but 'were not good, & were very restricted'. Thus, on their last night before another tour in the trenches, the Middlesex men were ill served and uncomfortable.

They did not have to endure their discomfort for long, as next day they were up before dawn to begin their march to the trenches at 6.00 am. They relieved the 2nd Dismounted Battalion, made up of men from the 9th Lancers and the 4th Dragoon Guards, completing relief at 10.00 am. The trenches were in a poor condition and in need of many repairs. In places the fire-steps were non-existent, and forward of the firing line the wiring was 'very poor & scanty'. If that first morning back at the front was quiet, it was just the calm before the storm, for Aby and the Middlesex men were on the very brink of a very fierce but almost forgotten encounter known as the Battle of the Craters.

Two platoons from B Company were posted to the front line trenches known as Bigger Willie – a reference to Kaiser Wilhelm – with a trench elsewhere called Little Willie – a snipe at the Kaiser's son. From events that follow it is probable that Aby was one of the soldiers posted to Bigger Willie. Another B Company platoon was put in Gordon Alley – a support line trench – and the last in Anchor trench. To the left of the Middlesex men were the 7th Royal Sussex, and the Dismounted Battalion to the right. It appears likely that the 11th Middlesex were opposed by the 23rd Bavarian Infantry Regiment, who at 3.30 pm received the 'benefit' of a bombardment by British heavy artillery.

The German front line was damaged, and they retaliated with trench mortar and rifle grenades. For Aby, his eighteenth tour of the trenches was one tour too many, and with three of the rifle grenades exploding close to him, he was deafened and severely shaken. He was sent to the dressing station at about 6.00 pm, but in the darkness, and with his nerve severely shattered, he could not find it. The fact that he was sent, rather than decided to go of his own volition, is supported in that the War Diary does not list any men as missing for 12 February. The frightened boy found himself in the shattered remains of Vermelles, where he sought and found refuge with some men of the Royal Field Artillery.

Though little remained above ground, Vermelles was built with strong cellars, and in several places a sub-terranean oasis could be found. The Army Chaplain, H.W. Blackburne speaks of one such place, where a man could rest comparatively secure from the noise of battle.

I have found up at Vermelles a glorious place for a Divisional Club, where we can have tea and buns for the men going in and out of the trenches. It is a huge cellar under a brewery which has been knocked to bits; but the cellar is alright ...

The Cellar Club is now in full swing. At one end is the bar for buns, tea and cigarettes. I have found a baker in Bethune and have taught him how to make English penny buns.

Aby spent the night in the cellars of Vermelles, but did not linger long, being up early next morning in time to walk the three kilometres to Sailly Labourse by 8.30 am. Aby reported to Company Quartermaster Sergeant W. Simpson. Aby was still in full trench order and was carrying his rifle. He told CQMS Simpson that he was suffering from shock from the explosion of a rifle grenade and Simpson observed him to be in a nervous condition. He took Aby to the Quartermaster, and then to Captain J.H. Ward of the Royal Army Medical Corps. Captain Ward said that Aby was fit for duty in the trenches and he was taken back to the Quartermaster. At 10.00 or 10.30 am, the Quartermaster ordered Aby to return to the trenches and gave him a note. He told Aby that it would be a serious matter if he failed to report himself back to his company.

Aby left Battalion HQ in the direction of the trenches. We can only imagine the conflicts tearing at his mind. He is a soldier. He has his duty to do. He knows that to do anything else is a serious thing. He is a seventeen-year-old boy. He has seen much death and experienced life that would weigh down a man's soul. With a quartermaster's order ringing in his ears he sets out for the trenches, but at precisely this time, the Germans begin a heavy bombardment. Had the heavy artillery laid off for just a little longer maybe he would have rejoined his company. But if the dreadful conflict within Aby's mind needed the scales to be tipped, the enemy barrage of those very lines to which he was supposed to go, must have been more than sufficient. At some time around 10.30 am, Aby turned his back on the trenches and walked the other way.

The records show that by midday at the latest, Aby was back at the farmhouse in La Flandrie. That is a straight-line distance of eighteen kilometres, or eleven and a quarter miles, which Aby is supposed to have covered in a maximum of two hours. Either evidence given to the court martial was erroneous, or Aby completed the journey otherwise than by foot. It is possible he lorry-hopped, jumping on the back of an ASC truck, but such a tactic would be unlikely to take him to a former billet, especially one as off the beaten track as the farmhouse at La Flandrie.

There is one way that Aby could have covered the distance in the given time though. The railway line that passed through Bethune went on towards Lillers. Once through Lillers it passed within three-quarters of a kilometre of the farmhouse. Of course there is no stop, but it would be possible to jump from the train, an action that would explain something else. When seen at the farmhouse, Aby was described as being covered in mud and without his cap and greatcoat.

The account of events that follows is at least a strong possibility, and one of the few explanations possible if the times mentioned in the court martial are to be believed. It has to be said that Aby himself contested the times, and this was backed up by evidence given by Madame Cordionne. Neither Aby's account nor Madame Cordionne's evidence was reliably refuted and so the following explanation is being generous to the court martial.

Aby left the trenches behind him, frightened and with his mind in turmoil. With his nerves in tatters he headed for Bethune. Wandering around for a while trying to get his head straight, he thought of the only place he had known any true respite since his arrival in France – the farmhouse at La Flandrie. It was cold and wet, and thoughts of that fireplace helped him to decide his next move. He hopped on a train – the kilometres were soon eaten up. He either got off at Lillers and walked the rest of the way, or, given the state of his uniform, jumped the train as it passed close to the village of La Flandrie. By noon, or as early as 11.00 am, Aby was sharing that fire with men of the 6th Buffs, chatting and trying to dry off. He certainly did not 'hide in a barn' as some other accounts suggest.

As he tried to get warm and dry he must have known it was just a matter of time before his presence among the Buffs would be questioned. His respite would last but a few short hours and his freedom would swiftly come to an end.

Chapter 11

Court Martial

You can't believe that British troops 'retire'
When hell's last horror breaks them, and they run,
Trampling the terrible corpses – blind with blood.
                                        Siegfried Sassoon

Aby joined in conversation with the men of the 6th Buffs and at some point spoke with Madame Jeanne Cordionne. While he was trying to get dry, the Bavarians were attacking the 11th Middlesex with trench mortars, rifle grenades and heavy artillery 'doing a considerable amount of damage & causing casualties'. As time was running short for some of the men in the trenches, so too were Aby's seven hours of shelter by the farmhouse fire. At about the same time as No. 5 Company of the 2nd Battalion, 23rd Bavarian Infantry were charging the trench called 'Bigger Willie', Corporal Edwin Lafont of the 6th Buffs was becoming suspicious of the dishevelled young soldier by the fireside.

B Company of the 11th Middlesex repelled the German attack with bayonet and bomb close to the time when Corporal Lafont arrested Abraham Harris and took him to the Company commander. Monday, 13 February 1916 had been a bad day for Aby, and also for his Battalion, who lost ten men to enemy action with forty-nine others wounded. Five men were listed as missing, one of whom must have been Aby. He was put under guard, probably at the HQ of the 6th Buffs, and was returned to his own battalion at Sailly Labourse two days later.

Sometimes when soldiers were arrested for desertion, they were not confined until their court martial, as this was seen to be keeping them out of harms way while their comrades were facing all the

116

dangers of the front line. In other cases they were confined from the time of their arrest right up until their execution. There is circumstantial evidence to suggest that up until charge at least, Aby may have fallen into the former category. Aby writes home of his troubles only on 23 February – a date which coincides with his battalion's first spell in proper billets after their tour of the trenches, and which was immediately followed by the need for working parties to mend trenches and carry out other repairs. Had Aby been confined for all that time, it seems likely he would have written home a lot sooner. In fact, the opening line suggests that Aby may have written one earlier letter, but that he made no mention of his predicament.

23rd February 1916
Dear Mother,
    I have sent you a letter that I have received the parcel. I am well, hoping all of you are quite well.
    Dear Mother, we were in the trenches, and I was ill, so I went out and they took me to the prison, and I am in a bit of trouble now and won't get any money for a long time. I will have to go in front of a Court. I will try my best to get out of it, so don't worry. But, dear Mother, try to send some money, not very much, but try your best. I will let you know in my next how I got on. Give my best love to Mother, Father and Kate.
    From your loving son, Aby.

This was the last letter the Bevistein family ever received from Aby. They had no more word of him until April, and one can only imagine their anguish. And even then, when news came, it was the worst there could possibly be.

    Lieutenant Colonel Ingle was for some reason away from his battalion on 26 February – three days after Aby sent his last letter home – for Aby was brought before Major W.H. Samuel who was at that time commanding the 11th Middlesex, if only for a very short period. Aby was charged as follows.

When on active service deserting His Majesty's Service in that he, at SAILLY LA BOURSE, on the thirteenth of February 1916 – when ordered to return to the trenches absented himself from 11th (Service) Battalion Middlesex Regiment until apprehended at LA FLANDERIE on the same day.

117

The Battle of the Craters carried on, and other young men of the Battalion were reaching the end of their endurance. One such was nineteen-year-old No. 335 Private Henry Carter. Two days after Aby's charge was put to him an intense barrage was to begin, which would continue for days, and result in Henry and several other men following in Aby's footsteps — that is, in the opposite direction to the enemy. For Henry and for many other men of the Battalion, the lure of those cellars below the ruins of Vermelles was too much in the face of such mayhem, and like Aby, they reached a point where they could stand no more. The discipline of the 11th Middlesex was beginning to suffer and Brigadier General Boyd-Moss knew that something would have to be done about it.

Boyd-Moss's 36 Brigade had been assigned to take control of craters not yet in existence, but which the men of 107th Tunnelling Company, Royal Engineers were working hard to create. They were digging out four mines in the Hohenzollern sector, and the plan was that all four would be blown simultaneously so that the British could gain command of the German trenches. The charges placed in the main three mines were the largest ever used by the British up to that time.

On 4 March 1916, six days after Aby was charged, a court martial was convened near Divisional HQ which was now at the town of Noyelles, two kilometres south along the road from Sailly Labourse. In peacetime, it was the General Court Martial that stood as the highest judicial tribunal of the British Army. In time of war however, serious charges overseas were heard before the much more easily convened Field General Court Martial (FGCM). The rules were that an FGCM was to comprise at least three officers, at least one of whom, the president, whenever possible should hold the rank of major or above. They had the power to award any sentence that was open to a General Court Martial, but could only impose a death sentence if all members were in agreement.

The president at Aby's court martial, and that of Private Harry Martin of the 9th Essex who was tried on the same day, was Major G. Arbuthnot of the 5th Berkshire Regiment. Also sitting in judgement was Captain A.J. Vaux, also of the 5th Berkshire, and Lieutenant O.C. Harvey of the 7th Norfolk Regiment. Arbuthnot and Vaux were both officers in battalions attached to 36 Brigade – the same as Aby's 11th Middlesex – and Lieutenant Harvey was a 35 Brigade man. With the 12th Division and all its brigades involved in battle, and all the officers on the panel probably fresh from the front, it is hard to see how Privates Harris and Martin did not start the proceedings with a stripe against them.

Aby and Harry Martin were not tried together, but almost definitely one immediately followed the other. Certainly the administrative authorities of the Army soon started treating the two separate hearings as if they were one, cutting down on the paperwork and erroneously filing comments pertaining to Aby in Martin's case file. They were tried separately, but thereafter were treated as a pair, right up to and including their executions, and as we shall see, it is entirely possible that this slap-dash attitude helped rob Aby of a second chance which many like him were afforded. This should not be taken to imply that the court martial itself was anything but correctly conducted by the standards of the time.

That given, it may surprise the reader to learn that in a trial for his life, Aby was not represented by a defending officer or 'prisoner's friend'. This was not unusual, for although it was the prisoner's right to choose an officer to fulfil such a role, many accused soldiers were unaware of it and it was not part of the court's duty to inform him. Others chose not to avail themselves of an officer to speak on their behalf, choosing instead to defend themselves. Still others pleaded not guilty to the charges, but then failed to defend themselves, merely remaining silent throughout, neither cross-examining witnesses, nor making a statement. Aby, we will see, did cross-examine witnesses, but only those who did not hold the King's Commission. It is hardly surprising that a seventeen-year-old boy would find it virtually impossible to gainsay any evidence put by officers.

If the numerical order of the court martial files is an indicator, Aby's hearing followed that of Private Martin. Aby was marched before the court without hat or belt (if tradition was followed) and the preliminaries were attended to. The first witness was called, and that was CQMS Simpson. He testified as follows, the evidence being taken down in pencil by Major Arbuthnot.

At about 8.30 am on 13th February I was at SAILLY LA BOURSE. The accused reported to me and said he had been sent from the trenches about 6 pm on the 12th February, that he could not find the dressing station and had stayed in VERMELLES for the night with some RFA men. The accused's

Company was in the trenches at the time. The accused was dressed in trench order & had his rifle with him.

I took the accused to the Quartermaster, and then I took him to the nearest medical officer, Captain Ward R.A.M.C. The medical officer marked the sick report 'Duty' and stated he was fit for duty in the trenches.

I took the accused back to the Quartermaster about 10 or 10.30 am. The Quartermaster ordered the accused in my presence to proceed to the trenches and report to the adjutant; he gave the accused a note.

The Quartermaster remarked on the seriousness of the offence if he failed to report himself.

The accused went away in the direction of the trenches.

I next saw the accused on 15th Feb when he returned under escort.

The court asked CQMS Simpson for some detail about why Aby said he had absented himself, and for a comment as to his appearance. Simpson answered:

When the accused reported to me at 8.30 am he told me he had been sent from the trenches suffering from shock from a rifle grenade. He seemed in a nervous condition.

Aby declined to cross-examine the high ranking NCO. It is pertinent to Aby's condition and state of mind that he still appeared to be 'in a nervous condition' some twelve to fourteen hours after his close encounter with a clutch of grenades.

The second witness for the prosecution, Captain J.H. Ward, RAMC was called. He told the court that he had examined Aby and that he had found him 'suffering from no appreciable disease and marked him fit for duty'. He commented that Aby did not strike him as suffering from nerves at the time. The court asked Captain Ward of what Aby had complained when examined. He replied:

When he came to me, the accused said he was suffering from deafness caused by the explosion of a rifle grenade.

The third witness was No. 114 Corporal Edwin Lafont of the 6th Buffs (East Kents). The reader is asked to pay especial attention to the times mentioned in Lafont's evidence and to bear in mind that his evidence places Aby eighteen kilometres away from the position stated by the previous witnesses.

> On 13th February at about 11 am at LA FLANDRIE I saw the accused in the farm house where I was billeted. I asked him where his regiment was, he said 'I do not know. I lost it'. He had previously told me that his regiment was the 11th Middlesex and that he was going to join his regiment.
>
> I asked him where his regiment was & he told me it was at SAILLY LA BOURSE. He told me he had just come out of hospital. He had no greatcoat or hat and was covered with mud.
>
> He stayed in the farm all the afternoon, sitting by the fire warming himself. He talked to the other men.

The next two lines of evidence have been scribbled out and are illegible. Major Arbuthnot has initialled the amendment. This appears to be the result of a successful piece of cross-examination by Aby that rendered these two lines inadmissible. The Corporal continues:

> At about 7.30 pm I again asked him where his regiment was, and he said it was in the trenches. I arrested him and took him before my Company officer.
>
> I know SAILLY LA BOURSE. LA FLANDRIE is near LILLERS. It is further away from the trenches than SAILLY LA BOURSE and in the opposite direction.

Aby cross-examined Lafont over a matter of hearsay. He answered:

> I did not myself hear you tell the men in the billet anything about your regiment.

The court asked Corporal Lafont about the location of La Flandrie, and he told them it was about a quarter of an hour's walk from Lillers. Aby then put it to the Corporal that it was 3.30 pm when the Corporal first saw him, and not 11.00 am. The Corporal stuck to his guns, saying:

> It was not 3.30 pm when I first saw the accused. It was between 11 and 12 o'clock.

121

In the last chapter, a scenario was described whereby the times mentioned by CQMS Simpson (10.00 to 10.30 am) and Corporal Lafont (between 11.00 am and 12 noon) could both be correct. If Aby had hopped on a train he could have covered the distance in the time available, thereby reconciling these two otherwise incompatible pieces of evidence. It was the evidence of the next witness for the prosecution that throws doubt on the correctness of the times mentioned by Lafont and tends to support Aby's piece of cross-examination.

The prosecution called Jeanne Cordionne, the owner of the farmhouse at La Flandrie. If, as is suspected, her name was spelt incorrectly in the court martial papers, she may be one and the same as the Jeanne Cordonnier whose tomb is located in the neighbouring communal cemetery at Busnes and who lived from 1887 to 1973. She had not been shown on the summary of evidence and that being the case, Aby had the right to object to her being called. The court informed him of this right, but he did not object to her giving evidence. In the event, her evidence proved particularly damning. The fact that it did not support the times mentioned in Lafont's evidence is an interesting anomaly, but at the end of the day, was of little relevance to the charge.

> I live at the farm at LA FLANDRIE, which is about 2 kilometres North of LILLERS.
>
> I recognise the accused. He came to the farm on Sunday 13th February. He arrived between 3 & 4 in the afternoon.
>
> I recognise him as he had been billeted in the farm for 3 weeks in January.
>
> He said the Germans had been bombing our trenches and he had left them, and was going to England. I told him he was to go back to the trenches. I am sure he said what I have stated. I have not misunderstood him.

Aby cross-examined Madame Cordionne, asking her what they had spoken about. She replied:

> I asked the accused about a few fellows I knew.

Thus concluded the case for the prosecution. Aby's defence comprised nothing more than his own statement. He took the oath and gave his side of the story.

I left the trenches because 3 rifle grenades exploded near me and I was deafened & my nerves had gone a bit. The Quartermaster sent me to Captain Ward, RAMC, and he passed me as fit for duty and told me I was fit for the trenches.

The Quartermaster told me to report to the Adjutant and gave me a note for him. He told me to return to the trenches and warned me that it was a serious thing not to go back.

I felt nervous and lost my head. I wandered round the town towards Bethune. I went through Bethune into La Flandrie thinking to stop there for a few days and then to return to my regiment.

The prosecutor (possibly Captain Pargiter, as the duty of prosecutor often fell to the adjutant of the prisoner's own unit), cross-examined Aby. The questions may be surmised from the answers Aby gave. He said:

I understood the Quartermaster's orders to me to return to the trenches.

I knew I was going in the opposite direction to the trenches.

I meant to go to the farm at La Flandrie and stay there for a few days.

I did not intend to return until the Company came out of the trenches.

I deny telling Madame Cordionne that I intended to return to England.

Aby had completed his case for the defence, but in reality it was no case at all. As for Madame Cordionne, was her command of English so good that there was no chance of her misunderstanding Aby? Could she have mistaken 'I want to go home' for 'I am going home'? It matters little, for even if her contribution to the case was entirely scrubbed out, Aby had convicted himself by his own mouth. The offence of desertion would be complete if it could be proved that the accused had effected an unauthorized absence with the intent of avoiding a 'particularly important service'. It was not a requirement that the accused intended to stay away from his unit forever. In fact, duration of absence did not form any part of the offence.

Aby had told the court, 'I did not intend to return until the Company came out of the trenches', and that was enough. Had the court officials wished to assure themselves that Aby knew what he was saying, they could have expanded on the prosecutor's question and asked Aby as to the nature of the duty he sought to avoid. But why complicate matters? FGCMs were designed to be short affairs and legal niceties were best left with clever lawyer chappies back in Blighty. Aby had told the truth. His evidence is virtually identical to that of the prosecution witnesses. Part of that truth amounted to admitting almost all the elements required to secure a conviction. Another part of that truth spoke of illness and shock, and even admission to hospital. Whereas the former was not missed and was used to convict, the latter was never mentioned again, although it was surely important in terms of post-conviction mitigation, not to mention Aby's intent and state of mind. 'Intent' was a vital element to the offence, and yet it was scarcely examined.

The evidence for the prosecution and the defence having been laid before the board, they would have taken very little time to come to a decision. Aby would have been marched out while the court considered its verdict. Unlike many men, Aby was then marched back to hear the finding.

Aby was found guilty as charged, and the words must have struck him like a physical blow. It was a known fact to the men of the British Army that a finding of guilt in a desertion charge often led to a death sentence. If he was still capable of taking anything in, the words of his platoon commander must have given some cause for hope. His officer now was none other than Arthur Redford, who had enlisted as a private soldier a few days before Aby. He reported that Aby's Army Form B122 – the personal discipline sheet – was unavailable as it was locked up with Battalion papers in the trenches. He then said:

The accused was in my platoon. He bears a good character. When the Battalion came out the accused begged to be allowed to come with it. It was intended to leave him behind, but he was very anxious to come out.

124

Aby – probably in a state of shock – did not ask any questions. The papers do not record whether the court asked if he had anything to say before sentence was considered. He was marched out, and although the sentence was undoubtedly passed in moments, he would not hear it until 19 March. A sentence of death was not official until approved by the GOC British Forces.

It is likely that from this time onwards Aby was kept in confinement in a conveniently secure place near to Brigade or Divisional HQ. Maybe he shared a makeshift cell with Harry Martin. Certainly their paperwork was now lumped together, and unfortunately for Aby, it was Martin's file that was then sent 'upwards' through the various general ranks. It appears someone decided to lessen their own work burden by reducing admin, and the required post-court martial paperwork has been adapted to show both Aby and Harry Martin's paperwork in a single file, instead of each of them having a set in separate files. This would have been of little consequence had Aby and Harry been of similar character. They were not.

An examination of court martial files of the period reveals a standard pattern of paperwork. After the finding, Army Form A3 is usually present which comprises four points covering (a) the guilty man's character, both in general and as a fighting man, (b) a statement as to whether the crime was deliberate or not, (c) a comment as to the discipline of the man's unit and (d) any reason that the sentence should not be carried out. This form is usually completed by the man's brigadier general. It is attached to the file, which is then passed up to the major general commanding the division, then to the lieutenant general commanding the corps and then to the general commanding the army. All of these add comments as to their opinion and recommendation. In this case the file went to Field Marshal Haig who appended his decision. None of these papers or decisions are to be found on Aby's file. They are all on Harry Martin's and their detail is as follows.

Reference 12th Divn. No. C.M. 370-371, dated 6.3.16.
Army Form A 3 completed as directed in both cases.
As Regards the case of No. 21161 Pte. H. MARTIN, 9th Essex Regt.-
(a) Prisoner had only served five days at the front in Second Line, and had no opportunity of displaying fighting proclivities.

He is a dirty, ignorant soldier with a very indifferent character and bad antecedents

(b) C.O.s statement attached. He is of the opinion that the crime was deliberate.

(c) Good.

(d) I can see no reason for recommending that the sentence not be carried out.

As regards the case of No. 1799 Pte. A. HARRIS, 11th Middlesex Regt.-

This man belongs to the 36th Brigade, the Brigadier of which must reply to (a), (b) and (c).

As regards (d), I can see no reason for recommending that the sentence be not carried out

8/3/16

Brigadier-General
Commanding 35th Infantry Brigade

The Brigadier General of 35 Brigade was Solly-Flood, and there can be little doubt that he seriously harmed Aby's chance of receiving a commuted sentence. As he points out himself, Aby was not of his brigade, so he had no grounds for answering 'd' above in the way he did. In the event, there are no comments on file by Brigadier General Boyd-Moss, the officer commanding 36 Brigade. Instead there are some comments by Lieutenant Colonel Ingle, commanding the 11th Middlesex. His comments are in pencil, are dated 8/3/16, and appear in Harry Martin's file:

(a) The character of No 1799 Private A HARRIS from a general point of view is indifferent. His conduct in the field is bad. He always tries to get out of the way if any operations are in progress, and cannot be trusted.

(d) I consider the crime was deliberate.

Underneath this someone has added:

The G.O.C. 36th Inf Bde states that the discipline of the Battalion is 'fair'.

This comment is also dated 8/3/16. In the margin next to the Lieutenant Colonel's remarks, someone has written in pencil:

But see character given by his platoon commander (p6).

The 'page 6' in question is the page 6 in Aby's own file, whereas the note is in the file of Private Martin. Page 6 of Martin's file is of no relevance to Aby or his character. Judging by the comments appended to Martin's file 'on the way up' and which are applicable to both Martin and Aby, it can only be concluded that the authors of those comments did not read what Aby's platoon commander had to say about him.

Before moving on to these comments, we should take some time to consider those of Lieutenant Colonel Ingle. It is strange that his opinion of Aby is so different to that of his platoon commander. Ingle's description of Aby's character as 'indifferent' is hard to reconcile with Lieutenant Redford's 'he bears a good character'. It is also hard to see how a battalion's commanding officer, responsible for in the region of a thousand men, would know a private soldier better than the man's platoon commander, in command of about fifty. There are only two explanations. Either Redford's opinion of Aby was incorrect and Ingle did in fact know better, or, Redford's opinion was correct and Ingle had another cause to report on Aby so unfavourably.

Let us break down Ingle's comments and consider the main elements. He stated that Aby's character in general was 'indifferent'. That is, his character was neither good nor bad. This is likely to mean that Aby was not a soldier who stood out from the crowd. He was not one known to volunteer, but nor was he a man who appeared on the defaulter's list.

He said Aby's conduct in the field was bad. Does this mean he was not a particularly skilled soldier? It cannot mean he disobeyed orders or infringed any other military requirements, because if so he would certainly have had a bad discipline record.

Finally, Ingle said that Aby 'always tries to get out of the way if any operations are in progress, and cannot be trusted'. Again, if this was true, why did Aby have a good record? How would Aby have come to be noticed in such a way as to lead his commanding officer to say such things of him? Could it be that Lieutenant Colonel Ingle remembered Aby's efforts to be granted leave for the Jewish holiday at the end of September 1915? Aby made an application, which resulted in the chaplain giving the Captain (Pargiter, the Adjutant?) a note, formalizing the request. How was Aby to know the launch of the Battle of Loos would correspond so closely with Passover? There is evidence that applications for, and granting of, leave for Jewish soldiers caused some resentment. George Coppard commented on it.

> There was only one person I knew whose professed religious beliefs did him any good, and that was a Jew named Levinsky. He came to our company on a draft, and had only been with us for about four weeks when he was given a week's leave in Blighty to attend ceremonies in connection with the Passover. It is not difficult to imagine the feelings of the Gentiles in the company who had been in France for a year with no leave, or hope of any, in the foreseeable future.

It cannot be discounted that Ingle's only cause to remember Aby's name was in connection with his application and that this coloured his opinion of the boy. What about the matter of trust? Well, all letters from Tommies were read by an officer before being sent on their way. Maybe the line in his last letter home, 'I will try my best to get out of it' was read. Perhaps the line rankled and added to Ingle's negative feelings.

We shall never know the true reasons behind Ingle's comments, but it is absolutely clear, if Aby had any chance of a commuted sentence, his colonel's comments had put paid to it.

Harry Martin's file went up to Major General Scott commanding 12th Division, leaving Second Lieutenant Redford's talk of Aby's good character in Aby's own file, quite clearly never to see the light of day again. There is no suggestion that this was a deliberate act, merely sloppy and corner-cutting. Scott's comments were brief and to the point.

> I consider these cases are deliberate ones of avoiding duty in the trenches and that the extreme penalty should be carried out.

Then it was the turn of the Lieutenant General commanding the Corps.

I strongly recommend that in both cases the sentence should be carried out. The aim in both cases was deliberate and there are a great many of these cases now occurring in the Corps.

This only left General Monro, commanding the First Army, who, from his words, clearly had not examined the case properly. Applying his oft used phrase 'worthless soldiers' he sealed the fate of both soldiers thus:

I recommend that the sentences awarded by F.G.C.M. on Pte Martin 9th Bn Essex Regt and Private Harris 11th Bn Middlesex Regt be carried into effect. They seem from mention to be both thoroughly worthless soldiers.

Having almost completed its journey upwards, Martin's file was reunited with Aby's and their respective blue front-sheets received the initials of Field Marshal Douglas Haig, confirming the sentences. Private Harry Martin and Private Abraham Harris were as good as dead.

Chapter 12

Execution

Hark, I heard the bugle crying,
And where am I?
My friends are up and dressed and dying,
And I will dress and die.

A.E. Houseman

On Sunday, 5 March 1916, the day after Aby's court martial, nine-teen-year-old Henry Carter together with a large but unspecified number of Middlesex men were rounded up in the cellars of Vermelles by men of another 12th Division battalion, on the orders of Brigadier General Boyd-Moss. Of all the men arrested, only five were to be selected for trial by FGCM, and of those five only Carter actually stood before a board. In his recommendation Boyd-Moss wrote:

> I recommend the sentence of Death on Private CARTER, 11th Battn. Middlesex Regiment be put into execution.
>
> He was one of a number of men of the 11th Middlesex Regt. who left the trenches without permission while a severe engage-ment was on. The Battalion was so disorganised that I ordered patrols of another battalion to search the cellars of VERMELLES on March 5th to arrest all men of the 11th Middlesex Regt. found hiding there. These men were afterwards sent to SAILLY.
>
> Five of the worst cases were selected for trial by F.G.C.M. There were numerous delays and four of the five men became ineffective.
>
> The <u>discipline of the battalion is not good</u>, and I think it necessary to make an example of this man.

Douglas Haig underlined the text of the recommendation as shown and added a terse comment, 'Who commands it?' It is hard to see this as anything but a question mark over Lieutenant Colonel Ingle's abilities as a battalion commander. Perhaps Field Marshal Haig should have looked for other reasons why a previously commended battalion was going to the dogs. It was not just the men who had weathered months in mud-filled trenches, always in Death's shadow, but the officers too. Ingle was not immune from the attrition to morale that his battalion had been through.

Although the recommendations of Boyd-Moss in relation to the fate of Private Carter were not written until 13 April, the events that led to them, and the apparent disorder within the 11th Middlesex, were extant a fortnight before Aby's execution. They happened prior to Ingle's comments about Aby, so perhaps Aby was also required for the sake of example.

While his papers ascended, step by step, up the general ranks, Aby was most likely confined at Sailly Labourse, somewhere close to Brigade HQ. It is strange that he wrote no more letters home, but then his letters all shared one common theme – an overriding wish to put his mother's mind at ease. Maybe he wanted to wait until he heard news of his sentence before writing, in the hope that he could send her good news. It is very doubtful he had any inkling of his fate.

Fifty-nine men had already been shot for desertion at this stage of the War, but had they not been away from their battalions for weeks, been caught in civilian clothing or attempting to board ships for Blighty? In comparison, Aby must have thought his offence quite slight. After all, he had served in the trenches for seven months and had earned the right to wear a wound stripe. It may have surprised him that a few had been shot for offences the details of which were no more serious than his. But what about Second Lieutenant Redford's comments? Aby would have been aware of these as unusually, they were made in front of the board with Aby present. Aby declined the opportunity to comment on his officer's assessment of him. He would have had no idea of the adverse comments made from there on up the chain of command. It may have surprised him even more that there were cases of men whose reputations were lauded by brigadiers and lieutenant generals, only for their recommendations for commutation to be ignored further up 'for the sake of example'.

Following the common practice in dealing with condemned men at the time, Aby was not told of his sentence until the day before the execution. His sentence was 'promulgated and extracts taken' on the evening of Sunday, 19 March 1916, by the Adjutant of the 11th Middlesex, Captain (soon to be Major) L.L. Pargiter. In other words, Aby – probably together with Harry Martin – was read extracts from the court martial papers and officially informed that he would suffer death by shooting at dawn on the next day. An army chaplain of the First World War, Julian Bickersteth, recorded the form of a typical promulgation in his diary. He writes of speaking with the Senior Chaplain who had intended to take on the task of seeing a condemned man through from promulgation to execution. However, Julian knew the man and felt it his duty to give such comfort as was possible. He went down to the Transport Lines where he saw the firing party.

These men had been sent down specially from the trenches. I made several arrangements about the digging of the grave and then went on to the spot where the promulgation was to take place. This consisted of the prisoner being marched under escort to a spot just outside the village. Here he was placed in the centre of a hollow square formed by representatives drawn from each battalion in the Brigade. At a given signal the prisoner is ordered to take two paces to the front, which he does, and his cap is taken off, and then the officer in charge of the parade reads the sentence, which concludes with a recital of the crime for which the prisoner has been found guilty. I stood close behind the prisoner to support him by my presence all I could. There was a terrible silence when the promulgation concluded with the sentence of death. The man seemed a bit dazed, but stepped back to between his guard fairly smartly. I walked off the ground with him. He was taken to a little back room on the second storey of a semi-detached villa in the village.

It is hard to imagine the mental anguish Aby must have suffered through his last hours. Dread at the thought of approaching dawn. A numbness born of incomprehension, disbelief and the bizarre unreality of the situation. Tomorrow the sun would come up, and he would not see it. For some men, the lifting of all uncertainty concerning their future, made way for a feeling of calm acceptance. Some passed their last night with such self-possession and dignity that the men guarding them were reduced to tears. Others were so frightened that the guard would conspire to bring them alcohol so that drink could blunt the edges of their pain. Yet other men went through all the above extremes as night crept on and dawn drew nearer.

It is an uncomfortable feeling to empathize with Aby during his last hours, and an experience that cannot help but draw out an emotional response. The former chaplain, R.H.J. Steuart, eloquently describes the feeling in his book, *March, Kind Comrade*.

> To die amongst the roar and in the shock and fury of battle is a thing that many men had come hardly to fear, and others almost to desire; but how frightful to be led out, blind-fold and bound in the chill of the morning, and there to be silently put to death – the very phrase is a strangling horror in itself.

In many cases, the chaplain stayed through the whole night with the condemned man, as did Julian Bickersteth. The man whom he friended to his death was under close guard, not just to prevent him escaping, but absurdly, to stop him committing suicide. Having ordered the nature of the man's death, it appears the generals would not be thwarted in their choice of method, even if death was the ultimate result.

> An appeal that the sentries might be removed is not accepted. There are no bars to the window and the prisoner might seek to make an end of himself. So I sit on silently. Suddenly I hear great heaving sobs, and the prisoner breaks down and cries. In a second I lean over close to him, as he hides his face in his hands, and in a low voice I talk to him.

Julian Bickersteth told the distraught man of all the fine fellows who had passed on and what company he would find on the other side. The man calmed down, but did not much wish to talk. He drank the tea brought for him and ate the bread and jam. Later, he asked if they could sing hymns, and beginning with 'Rock of Ages', the Chaplain and the condemned man sang many hymns together. He slept then, waking occasionally, until it was his time.

There is no known record of how Aby, or indeed the vast majority of the other 306 men (and boys) shot for military crimes, spent their last night. It is reasonable to assume that some few details may have been included in the Divisional War Diaries of respective Assistant Provost Marshals, but most of these are lost. It is believed these records were kept in damp conditions – away from the other documents that have survived and may be examined at the Public Record Office – and rotted away before reaching the time when they would have been available for public use. Maybe, in a dark corner of an attic, in the pages of a long-forgotten diary of a Jewish chaplain or an 11th Middlesex man, the secret of Aby's last night is still biding its time.

In the early hours of Monday, 20 March 1916, evidence suggests that Private George Coppard, now of the 37th Company Machine Gun Corps, was on sentry-go in Sailly Labourse where a crossroads is formed by the main road through the town, the Rue d'Annequin off to the east and the Rue de Noeux to the west. Both roads led to mines. The Annequin mine had been fixed up by the 23rd Sanitary Section to serve as a bathing centre. It could 'do about 100 per hour'. Unfortunately the facility often came under enemy fire and therefore was 'not as popular as it might be otherwise'. The road towards Noeux-les-Mines passed through Labourse first and then onwards to a disused mine.

What was Aby's last sight before the blindfold was tied across his brow? Perhaps the photo of his mother, which he kept close, held up for him by a sympathetic guard or chaplain. Was his mind so numbed that he was led, automaton-like, to the place where he was to be shot, or were his last thoughts clear? Did he believe in his own heart, that he deserved to die, and that his offence was so wicked that there could be no other outcome but death? Did he fight the inevitable, necessitating some kind of restraint, physical or chemical? Did he accept his fate and walk quietly to his death? Did he stumble to the place in disbelief, hopeful until the shots rang out that somehow he would be saved? These are not comfortable thoughts, and were this a purely historic account, they would be out of place. But in considering the life of one young man, it is valid to speculate upon the emotions he may have felt.

Aby and Harry Martin were executed at Labourse, probably taken there by motor ambulance from their places of confinement. George Coppard most probably speaks of Aby and Martin's firing party, in the following extract from his book.

> At Sailly I was put on guard duty. It was early November and the nights were dark and cold. Flashes of light from the Hohenzollern Redoubt five kilometres east lit the sky. I could hear the deep roar of minnie bursts as I paced up and down outside a row of miner's cottages in which my companions were sleeping. At first light in the morning a party of a dozen men approached my post and turned off into the Annequin road, where there was a disused coal mine. Later on I heard a volley of shots. A rumour went round that two Tommies had been executed that morning. Rumours of that kind were generally based on fact. Somebody always got to know.

Although Coppard states that the event occurred in November 1915, records show that no 'two Tommies' were executed at that time. Only one man was executed that month, and at another location. Coppard's battalion was at Sailly Labourse in November 1915, but his new unit was also there in March 1916. Of course, the nights would have been equally dark and cold at either time and when tested against the other documented evidence, it seems very likely he got the months mixed up, surely an easy mistake to make after the passage of so many years.

Taking this to be the most logical route for a firing party to march in order to get from Sailly Labourse to Labourse, one may walk the same route today and see that very little has changed. Near the crossroads is a derelict terrace of cottages that may well have been the ones in which Coppard's pals were sleeping. A brisk march towards Labourse and the now well-wooded slagheap that represents the location of the disused mine, one passes by old farm buildings that are changed from those days only by the ravages of time. Passing out of Sailly, the land is flat for miles around save only for the slagheap. After twelve or so minutes, the narrow metalled road passes over an embankment. Along the top of the embankment is a path that crosses the A26 via a footbridge. In Aby's day a railway track ran along the embankment towards the mine. Once over the ridge and clear of the scrubby growth of shrubs and small trees on its bank, Labourse Communal Cemetery comes into view.

The embankment, being the only relief to the flatness of the surrounding land and situated within a hundred yards of the place where Aby now rests, is the most likely site of the execution.

The form of executions at this time varied only in the detail. If a man had accepted sufficient alcohol he would have been insensible, and if this eventuality had been foreseen, it was often the case that he would be bound to a chair or strung up on the execution post like 'an alcoholic jelly'. Other men were marched blindfold to the post and co-operated with the man who had to affix the bindings. Almost invariably the medical officer would pin a paper disc or piece of rag on the man's tunic over his heart as an aiming point for the firing party. In the case of double executions, like Aby's, the men would be shot simultaneously, the men of the firing party being assigned a target.

There would have been a considerable entourage at the execution. Certainly Lieutenant Colonel A.C. Tompkins, 12th Division Assistant Provost Marshal (APM) was there as protocol demanded, and at least one chaplain would have been present. Battalion Adjutants, Captain Pargiter of the 11th Middlesex and Captain C.C. Spooner of the 9th Essex were probably there and Captain L. Meakin, RAMC, was the doctor present. Then, in addition to the officers and the firing party, there would have been the prisoner escorts and perhaps two or three military policemen.

R.H.J. Steuart describes a typical execution.

At a sign from the A.P.M., the firing party, which up till then had stood with their backs to the condemned man, faced about to him. At a second sign they took aim; at a third they fired: and the bound figure crumpled and slid down as far as the ropes would let him go.

Instantly the officer in command called his men to attention, formed fours, and marched them off; and the medical officer, stepping forward to examine the body, reported five bullets through the heart.

In a similar manner, Aby and Harry Martin met their end. Captain Meakin examined the boy and the man and pronounced life extinct. On a scrap of paper from a notebook, he wrote:

I certify that the death of No 1799 Pte A. Harris 11ᵗʰ Batt.
Middlesex Rgt took place at 5.29 am on March 20th 1916.

It is with trepidation one first notes that Captain Meakin did not
include the usual comment that 'death was instantaneous'. However,
in recording the exact same time of death on Harry Martin's death
certificate, it can be assumed with some degree of certainty that
neither suffered the horror of surviving the fusillade. Such cases did
occur, and then the officer in charge of the firing party would be
obliged to finish the job with his revolver.

The communal cemetery of Labourse was a short way from where
Aby's body was untied. Within the cemetery was a small plot
assigned to the Field Ambulance unit to bury men who had died of
wounds. Although it was not uncommon for Field Ambulances to put
those men they could not save into a communal grave, we know from
the War Graves Commission that Aby was put into an individual
grave. Free of the rope that had tied him to the post and free of the
bonds of life, Aby's remains were wrapped up in an army blanket and
lowered into the earth. The chaplain would have spoken a few words
of committal. Steuart's description of the aftermath of an execution
must hold true for Aby in many aspects.

> The cemetery lay a few hundred yards away; and in less than a
> quarter of an hour from the time that the dead man and I had
> sat talking together in the hut, the earth had been pressed down
> over him in his grave, and I was signing the label for the
> identifying peg at his head.
>   That, and a pool of bright red blood steaming in the hollow
> of the stretcher, was all the trace that he had left.

The identifying peg, a pool of bright blood and an aching emptiness
that would stay with his family forever. Abraham Bevistein's short life
was over, but his name was far from forgotten. Rebecca Bevistein in
particular, Aby's beloved mother, was never to get over the cruel loss
of her son. Like many thousands of mothers who had lost sons,
she grieved, but unlike the multitude, she could seek no solace or
comfort in friends or neighbours because her son had been executed,
and shame was a pain that had to be faced alone. Rebecca was struck
down by the news of her only son's ignoble death and she never
regained her health.

Chapter 13

Questions in the House

Every bullet has its billet;
Many bullets more than one:
God! Perhaps I killed a mother
When I killed a mother's son.

Sgt Joseph Johnstone
Black Watch

Back at Anthony Street, Joseph, Rebecca and Kate languished without news from Aby. They knew he was in trouble from his letter of 23 February, but then there was nothing more. As Aby had been such a regular correspondent, the Bevisteins were quite possibly expecting bad news, so when a letter came, not from Aby but from the War Office just before mid-April, their fears must have been raised considerably. Nothing could prepare them for the news it carried. Dated 8th April 1916, the terms of the letter are particlarly cold, but then, there was little careful wording could do to soften the blow.

> Sir,
>   I am directed to inform you that a report has been received from the War Office to the effect that No 1799 Private Harris, 11th Battalion Middlesex Regiment, G.S., was sentenced after trial by Court Martial to suffer death by being shot 'for Desertion', and the sentence was duly executed on 20th March, 1916.
>   I am, Sir, your obedient servant,
>   P.G. Hindley, 2nd Lieut

Quite naturally, the family were devastated. Rebecca's grief was completely overwhelming and she took to her bed, inconsolable.

Apart from breaking the awful news to the neighbours, it is unlikely Joseph or Kate felt able to go into the details. Nevertheless, there were whispers, and news of Aby's fate did get out and reached the ears of a young man whose name is lost to history. His was a small voice, but so incensed was he, that he sought out one whose words reached further, and by his actions Aby's name lives on.

He took Aby's story to Sylvia Pankhurst, a great champion for the ordinary people of the East End. Second daughter of the famous Emmeline Pankhurst, Sylvia was no less committed to worker's rights and women's suffrage. She was also very much against the War and strongly opposed conscription when it was introduced later in 1916.

Sylvia Pankhurst remembered the youth approaching her with 'the heavy sadness men wear in announcing ill-news'. He told her of five East End families who had received official news that a son of the household had been executed at the front, and that he wanted her to see the bereaved parents. She went with the youth, whom she described as 'one of those zealous young Jews to be found in all movements for popular advancement', to the Whitechapel area. There they met a second lad, and after some conversation, went on to 'a small, mean house in a side street'. Years later, Sylvia Pankhurst was to write a book, *The Home Front*, and in it would be a chapter devoted to Aby's story. She wrote of her meeting with Joseph, Rebecca and Kate, but their names are not mentioned.

> A middle-aged man, humble and sad, father to one of the lads who had been shot, led us to an upper room and silently motioned us within. The boy's mother lay on a bed there, too miserable to care for life, moving her head from side to side in the restless way of one who is ill with grief.
>
> The man and a young woman, who seemed his daughter, with hushed voices, now in English, now in Yiddish, told the story. The mother moaned and turned in her bed, as though each phrase of it were a stab to her.

Kate then brought out Aby's letters from the front. On a variety of scraps of paper, and written mainly in pencil, Sylvia Pankhurst read them and noticed that in nearly every one, Aby had expressed regret for the worry he had caused his family by joining up and concern for their happiness. In reading them she formed the opinion of Aby as 'a good son and kindly'.

Pankhurst was not immune to the grief that was so palpable in the Bevistein household and she was determined to do what she could. At the time she was the editor of a worker's weekly newspaper called *The Dreadnought* and in the issue dated Saturday, 22 April 1916 – published barely over a month after Aby's execution – his story was under the main headline on the front page; 'EXECUTED: EAST LONDON BOY'S FATE'.

It is chiefly through this article that Aby's words from the front have come to us. Although Pankhurst virtually reproduced the piece twenty years later as a chapter in her book, *The Home Front*, she omitted the dates of Aby's letters in this later work. They are shown in the newspaper, and are important in that they help place Aby into the correct location and setting. The story was illustrated by the Dutch political cartoonist Louis Raemaekers. His cartoon shows a soldier being subjected to 'Field Punishment No 1' above the line 'Europe: Am I not sufficiently civilised yet!'

After bringing Aby's words to her audience and telling his story such as she could without access to official records, her article is summarized.

> Thus, after ten months in the trenches, this lad was injured in a mine explosion and taken to hospital suffering from shock and wounds at the end of December. He was released on January 19th, and in the middle of February became ill and left the trenches. For this he was shot by order of court-martial.

At the time, Sylvia Pankhurst had no way of knowing that Aby had left the trenches on the very first day back after his hospitalization, or that he had been ordered back into an area that was undergoing a fierce bombardment. This would have been enough to tax the courage of even the most stalwart person, let alone a young soldier with memories of his last injurious experiences so fresh in his mind.

She then makes clear the intentions of her fellows:

> The conscientious objectors in their fight for peace and liberty of conscience, will direct the attention of civilised peoples to the inner workings of the military machine, and will put an end to the possibility of such tragedies as this.

It is a sad irony that in her efforts to draw Aby's story into the light of day, Pankhurst inadvertently caused the Bevisteins more pain, if that were possible. Having used Aby's letters to illustrate the lad's plight she then sought to press political momentum by passing these on to a Member of Parliament so questions could be raised in the House. It is the belief of Aby's living relatives that the letters were never returned to the family, and so bereft of their only son, they were denied the small comfort they may have derived from all those letters home. A search of many archives has failed to reveal any trace of them.

Sylvia Pankhurst published her story and then wrote to the War Office to protest against 'the cruel injustice of executing a young lad who had endured nearly eight months in the trenches, and so recently had lain three weeks or more in hospital for injuries and shock'. She also asked that his parents be allowed compensation in the form of a pension allowance. This was less than a forlorn hope and she could not have been surprised when this was refused.

It was not long before Aby's name was mentioned in the House in connection with the execution of British soldiers. It was far from being a new topic of inquiry. As far back as June 1915 there had been questions as to the number of men executed, the nature of the offences for which a sentence of death could be imposed, and later, how members of an executed man's family were informed of the death. But it was on 4 May 1916, six weeks after his death, that Aby's specific case was brought to the attention of the House.

Three died-in-the-wool socialists, having made themselves familiar with Aby's case, co-ordinated their questions to give the Under-Secretary of State for War (Mr Harold Tennant, Member for Berwickshire) an uncomfortable time. Frederick W. Jowett, Independent Labour Party Member for Bradford (West), loosed the opening shot. He wanted to know if Tennant would lay before the House the record of Aby's court martial and at the same time provide the names of the officers who made up the panel, and the officer or officers who confirmed the death sentence. Jowett also asked if the young soldier had been defended in any way, either by counsel, solicitor or prisoner's friend.

Tennant replied, 'It is regretted that it is not possible to comment upon the sentence of courts martial approved by the Commander-in-Chief.'

The answers to Jowett's questions would remain hidden away from the public at large for another seventy-five years, but on the day, Tennant's unrevealing reply was quickly followed by another question, this time from Philip Snowden, the Blackburn Member of Parliament who would go on to become Labour's first Chancellor of the Exchequer.

'Are we to understand from that reply,' he said, 'that it is or it is not a fact that this boy, only nineteen years of age, was shot?'

Tennant said, 'I don't know what his age was but undoubtedly he was shot.'

Tennant's reply, bordering on flippant, drew an indignant question from Robert Outhwaite, MP for Hanley. 'Is the Right Honourable Gentleman aware that the sentence of death was passed within a month of this boy leaving hospital where he had been for a nervous breakdown caused through wounds due to a mine explosion? Is it customary to shoot boys in such circumstances?'

The Under-Secretary's answer indicates that Outhwaite had hit him with information he had not anticipated.

'I was not aware of that fact … If there was any desertion …'

Outhwaite pressed on. 'If I show the Right Honourable Gentleman the letters I have received on this subject, will he take the matter into consideration?'

Probably embarrassed by the outflanking he had just suffered, all the more stinging as Robert Outhwaite was a member of his own party, Mr Tennant made no reply and the House was only the wiser for witnessing the questions. The sad fact was that it was very close to becoming customary to shoot boys. A week before these questions were raised, nineteen-year-old Henry Carter of the 11th Middlesex, who had left the trenches on the day of Aby's court martial, was shot at dawn. Of all those shot for military offences by the end of the War, almost 11 per cent were under twenty-one. It is interesting to note that Philip Snowden considered Aby a boy at nineteen. One wonders how the House would have received the news that he was in actual fact a month short of his eighteenth birthday.

Taken from a War Office file, the following comments were applied to named, executed soldiers. The names have been omitted here and only initials used. The file lists the thirty-two soldiers who were under twenty-one when executed. Aby is not on the list. The Army listed him as twenty-one years old at death, two years older than he should have been, even by Army reckoning.

Private I.R., aged twenty, 2nd Scots Guards.

> General character very good but he does not bear a good character as a fighting man.

Private G.R., aged nineteen, 2nd Kings Own York Light Infantry.

> Until recently he has been a good soldier, and bore a good character, but lately he seems to have lost his nerve.

Private A., 17th Royal Scots.

> Man was not a man who gave much trouble neither was he in any sense a man whom one would pick out as a good man. Considered to be of poor intellect, not much consideration as a fighting man.

Private S., 2nd West Riding.

> Always performed duty in trenches satisfactorily, man appears to be slightly deficient mentally.

Tennant was probably not best pleased when Aby's case was raised again, a week after its first airing in the House. On 9 May 1916, the Honourable Member for Blackburn addressed the House as follows:

> I have a case here ... of a lad who enlisted in the East End of London at the age of eighteen and a half years ... I have here copies of quite a considerable number of letters the lad wrote home to his mother at various dates from July of last year down to the end of January of this year. They are the letters not of a man, but of a boy. I do not know what the boy was physically, but every line in these letters indicates that they were written by a person whose mind was quite immature. What has happened to this boy?

Snowden went on to tell the House of Aby's injury and then of his execution, quoting from the War Office communications that his parents had been sent. He continued:

I have been repeatedly told from the Treasury Bench that no lad under twenty-one years is shot. This lad was shot, although the evidence goes to prove that his physical condition, and probably his mental condition, had been so much affected by the experiences through which he had passed that he was incapable of standing the continued strain of his military duties. It is to this you are exposing these lads of eighteen.

Later in the same sitting, Mr Nield made a further reference to Aby:

That a lad of eighteen should be called upon to face a firing party for desertion, and still more so in the case of an admitted shock due to a mine explosion. I am bound to say that is a thing which ought never to have occurred, and I hope sincerely that the military authorities will have such an investigation into the circumstances as to make it absolutely impossible for anything of that sort to happen again. When one remembers that the penalty is only exacted for the most atrocious crime in civil life and the most serious crime in civil life, I venture to think that the case ought never in any circumstances to have a repetition of it.

Aby's was not the first name mentioned in the House in connection with the executions, and it was not the last. Jowett, Snowden, Outhwaite and others had asked parliamentary questions before and they would continue to do so. The exchange these men had with the Under-Secretary did not have a profound effect nor did it alter the ways of the War Office, but together with Sylvia Pankhurst's publications, it did press Aby's name gently into the pages of history. Without Pankhurst, the author of *The Thin Yellow Line*, William Moore, would have been unable to write Chapter 7, 'Case of an East End Boy'. Without the publication of Aby's letters, few and incomplete as they are, there would be little upon which to base his story, and nothing to give those small insights into his character.

There is another interesting aspect to the fact that such questions were being asked while the War was still in progress. It puts paid to the argument that it is only in latter days that we look back with our modern sensibilities and find the practices of courts martial and the executions unacceptable. To many people they were unacceptable then, while they were still going on, and that the practices survived and outlived the War seems mainly attributable to the secrecy with which they were wrapped.

Seventy-six years later, Aby's name (this time followed by his own surname, albeit spelt incorrectly) was to stir lightly through the House once again, this time in the House of Commons' 'Written Answers'. Recorded in Hansard for 26 June 1992 is the following question and answer sequence:

Capital Sentences

Mr MacKinlay: To ask the Secretary of State for Defence how many requests have been received for review of capital sentences carried out under the British Army Acts between 1914 and 1920 in the latest period for which he has records.

Mr Archie Hamilton: Since 1989, the Ministry of Defence has received nine requests for pardons for soldiers executed during the First World War.

Private A. Beverstein

Mr MacKinlay: To ask the Secretary of State for Defence if he will place in the Public Record Office the War Office correspondence relating to the case of No. 11/1799 Private A. Beverstein (enlisted as Harris) of 11 Battalion of the Middlesex Regiment.

Mr Archie Hamilton: The War Office correspondence relating to this case is already available for inspection at the Public Record Office, primarily in class WO95, piece No. 1856, and in the court-martial file, WO71, piece 456, which was released to the public domain in January of this year.

So, Aby's name had spanned the decades in its own right, as well as appearing in schedules that mentioned all those who had been executed. In the years between the questions put by the likes of Frederick Jowett and Philip Snowden, and those written down by Andrew MacKinlay, Labour Member for Thurrock, the baton was taken up by several others, the most resolute perhaps being Ernest Thurtle.

Elected as the MP for Shoreditch in the 1923 elections, Thurtle had served as a captain during the War and his experiences led him to campaign for the abolition of the death penalty for cowardice and desertion. Many of his contemporaries in the House had served in the War and supported the campaign. Other backbenchers who had military experience did not.

When Thurtle reminded the House that there had been no evidence of a senior British military figure facing the death penalty since Admiral Byng during the Seven Years War of the mid-1700s, an elderly ex-military member called out that it was because they did not run away. Thurtle rejoined, 'They never get near the fighting line!'

Old soldiers they say, never die – they are replaced by other old soldiers. And so, even today there are those for whom the matter of the executed soldiers is quite simple. They ran away. And they got shot. So where is the problem? For another kind of old soldier, they saw the problem only too well and spent years in torment from having lost friends, or even worse, being ordered to form part of a firing party.

Chapter 14

A Sacrifice Less Worthy?

The universe is so vast and ageless that the life of one man can only be justified by the measure of his sacrifice.
Pilot Officer V.A. Rosewarne

The past is another land and no vessel can truly take us to that realm. There are, however, many 'charts and maps' that with careful study can provide us with a reliable impression of its geography. The charts and maps come to us in the form of primary source material, and are never more illuminating than when they reach us in the actual words of those who inhabited that unattainable world. In their book *Blindfold and Alone*, Cathryn Corns and John Hughes-Wilson say much the same.

> The sad fact is we cannot undo the past – we can only learn from it. Perhaps the best way of understanding what happened is to let the men who were there at the time speak for themselves.

This paragraph is then followed by a quote from someone who was 'there at the time'.

> When Miller disappeared just before the Hun attack, many of the men said he ... must have gone over to the enemy lines. They were bitter and summary in their judgement of him. The fact that he had deserted his commanding officer ... was as nothing to the fact that he had deserted them. They were to go through it while he saved his skin. It was about as bad as it could be, and if one were to ask any man who had been

through that spell of fighting what ought to have been done in the case of Miller there would only have been one answer. Shoot the bugger!

That the authors fail to mention the quote is not from a primary source, but from a novel first published in 1929, may be overlooked as the novel was written by a man who had served at the front as a private soldier. The fact that they chose to omit the very next line, which changes the whole context of the 'quote', is a little more difficult to forgive.

> But if that same man were detailed as one of the firing-party, his feelings would be modified considerably.

Later in the story, Miller, who escapes several times 'assumed heroic proportions' by escaping from a police tent with one NCO saying, 'That bugger deserves to get off.' The quote chosen by Corns and Hughes-Wilson is useful though, not because it gives a true indication of the prevailing thoughts at the time, but because it illustrates the folly in turning men over to the judgement of those still hot from battle. None are so contemptuous of those who have failed through giving up the fight than those who have prevailed through difficult odds. Reason and circumstance matter little. Objectivity is stripped away, and to condone or support the failure is to admit that possibility of failure in oneself.

We have laws to guard against subjectivity interfering with the cause of justice, and it is clear that courts martial were more often than not, kept within the framework of these laws. But when the law itself takes no account of reason or circumstance, when it is absolute, and 'swift' takes the place of 'sure', it is a poor law.

Maximilien Robespierre said:

> Any law which violates the indefeasible rights of man is essentially unjust and tyrannical, it is not a law at all.

How can the involuntary condition of losing ones nerve, in and of itself, amount to a capital offence in anything other than an unjust and tyrannical law? If then, following the loss of nerve a man deserts, having lost that ingredient so vital in helping him to overcome the natural instinct to survive, does that amount to so heinous

148

an offence that he deserves to die at the hands of his comrades? No argument could convince a sensible person to answer in the affirmative. But as Voltaire said of the execution of Admiral Byng, who was shot more to hide the inadequacies of King George II's lacklustre government then for failing to fully engage the French fleet:

> In this country it is thought well to kill an admiral from time to time to encourage the others.

Therein lies the key to the whole question. Were Aby and the other men and boys executed, such 'worthless' individuals that there was no place fit for them on the face of the earth? Of course not. Was Aby's crime so calculated, self-controlled and wicked that there could be no proper sentence other than death? Only the most callous and unfeeling would say so. Was it an evil necessity that he should die to 'encourage the others'? Perhaps it was.

Time and time again, the generals indicate in case files that the sentence should be carried into execution for the sake of example. It has to be said, leaving aside the moral arguments and looking from the pragmatic viewpoint, there is some validity to this stance. What could possibly persuade a man to endure day after day, the horrors of the trenches and the ever-present possibility of death, unless it be the certainty of death should one desert? Taking Aby's own battalion as an example, its discipline was crumbling and desperate measures were required to shore it up. Men were deserting in large numbers and even Field Marshal Haig had been made aware of the problem. Does this explain why Aby and Henry Carter had to die? The men of the 11th Middlesex needed a wake-up call. It was to come at dawn, in two instalments.

There were over three thousand death sentences handed down by courts martial during the War. Only 10 per cent of them were carried into execution. One is left only to wonder at the circumstances which led to 90 per cent of them being commuted, as only the papers of those executed have survived. How did Aby's case, which appears so trivial in comparison with others, carry on to the bitter end? Surely men could hardly be convicted on anything less, so why were their cases commuted and Aby's not?

It has to be considered that Aby died to save the Battalion's discipline. Was he indeed needed for the sake of example only? If that was the case, then surely his sacrifice is no less valid than that of other men who died in the trenches.

Henry Carter was in the same boat. Though not possessed of a good record, he was not executed for his past offences, and the one he did die for is hardly more serious than Aby's. Feeling unwell in the trenches near the Hohenzollern Redoubt, he reported to a sergeant and was given a note to go to the Field Ambulance. When he reached its last know position it had gone, so he cast around looking for it. He became wet through and went to the drying room in one of the cellars under the ruined town of Vermelles. He asked for, and was given, permission to stay there and dry out by the person in charge.

The next day he was arrested with a number of others, five of whom were charged with desertion. Only Carter was brought to trial. Even though it was admitted he had been given a note, and that the Field Ambulance had indeed moved, it was judged that Carter should have returned sooner to the trenches. In circumstances resembling those of the French Fusiliers of Vingré, of whom we will hear more in the last chapter, the nineteen-year-old was shot at 4.32 am on 26 April 1916. Dawn was coming earlier, but the shroud of secrecy surrounding the true nature of the executions was held tight shut and the British public was kept in the dark.

What of the soldiers themselves? George Coppard once again helps us to understand at least one viewpoint prevalent at the time.

> Prolonged exposure to siege warfare conditions of the type which prevailed in the Hohenzollern Redoubt seriously affected the morale and nervous systems of men not physically capable of endurance. If any poor devil's nerves got the better of him, and he was found wandering behind the lines, a not infrequent occurrence, it was prima facie a cowardice or desertion case ... It is my considered opinion that some men who met their end before a firing squad would willingly have fought the enemy in hand-to-hand combat, but they simply could not endure prolonged shell and mortar fire.

Aby rests in a row of three graves, surrounded by others. The three graves together are all those of men shot at dawn. This cannot be a coincidence. They lie towards the centre of a plot of seventeen British soldiers – one for each year of Aby's age – arranged in such a way

150

it appears that even in death, the deserters are under guard. There is Aby, and Harry Martin who was executed at the same time, and then there is Private William L. Thompson of the 6th Battalion, the Buffs. Looking at Thompson's case file, it appears he may well have been shot for deserting while suffering withdrawal symptoms from what is now a Class A controlled drug under the 1971 Misuse of Drugs Act. It further appears that the issue of these drugs was at the discretion of the MO and that he may have been taking them regularly.

William Thompson chose to submit a written statement in his defence, rather than give verbal evidence. His statement is still held within his case file.

I have been using Coca Extract for some considerable time …

These days we commonly know 'coca extract' by the name 'cocaine', a drug which produces a short feeling of intense euphoria followed by a debilitating and enervating depression, the intensity and duration of which increases with regular use.

He continued:

… and before going into the trenches this time instead of getting my usual allowance of it I received a letter instead informing me that I could not have any more of the drug without a Medical Officer's signature, the consequence was that I was extremely nervous & depressed before going into the trenches, but I had no intention of wilfully leaving the trench. When proceeding up the communication trench a shell landed almost on the parapet, the shock completely demoralising me so that I was hardly responsible for what happened afterwards. I have but a hazy idea of leaving the trench. I remember asking Sergt Page of A Coy if he would come to the dressing station with me as I had an idea that I could get something from the MO which would put me right, but Sergt Page said he could not. I must have got into a panic as I was wandering about Vermelles all that night and next day. I strove to pull myself together & go back to the trenches but it was useless my nerves were completely gone & I was in a state of abject fear. That night I proceeded down to our transport at Sailly La Bourse where I was arrested by the Company Quarter Master Sergt.

151

In an interesting letter attached to the file, an officer points out that Thompson's statement provides a good defence for any deliberate intention of deserting. It also points out that Thompson has a bad record and there is a very strong hint that it would be just as good to be rid of him, despite the defence.

So Aby rests – to his left, a soldier of the Royal Warwickshire Regiment and to his right, William Thompson who was also shot at dawn. To any casual visitor, there is nothing to differentiate between the sacrifice of any of the men who hold their ranks, shoulder to shoulder and stone to stone – and that is how it should be.

For our final airing of a voice from the past in this chapter, let us listen again to the words of Julian Bickersteth, the Chaplain, as he speaks of the second execution to which he was witness, from a letter home, as written on 29 December 1917.

> Once again it has been my duty to spend the last hours on earth with a condemned prisoner.

The man was Private Harry Williams of Queen Victoria's Rifles who, paralysed with fear during a German attack, had refused orders to join reinforcements.

> I cannot disclose to you many of the details of those trying hours, but I have, I hope, learnt much from the simple heroism of this mere lad of nineteen, who has been out here at the front since 1914 when he was only fifteen and a half, and in spite of two wound stripes on his arm and all that service behind him, has met his end. It was my privilege to comfort and help him all I could, to hear his first and last confession, to administer to him the Holy Communion and to stand by his side to the very end. We have no time here amid the stern realities of war for pathos. We could not live at all if we dwelt on the 'pathetic' side of this vast tragedy, but there are few deaths I have witnessed which so wrung my heart-strings as this one.
>
> He gave me all his little treasures to give to this or that friend. He wrote a letter to his sweetheart and sent her his letter wallet with its photographs and trinkets, a lucky farthing which she had given him for a keepsake, his last 'leave' ticket and other small things. He sent a letter to his best chum in the

regiment and said he was sorry he hadn't made good, and wished them all a happy New Year and hoped they would all get home safe after the war.

Of our more intimate time together I may not speak. He slept peacefully as a child for several hours. Just before the end I read to him very gently that hymn which will forever now have a new meaning for me and which was in every line and every word appropriate. 'Just as I am without one plea!' As they bound him, I held his arm tight to reassure him, – words are useless at such a moment – and then he turned his blindfolded face up to mine and said in a voice which wrung my heart, 'Kiss me, Sir, kiss me,' and with my kiss on his lips and, 'God has you in his keeping,' whispered in his ear, he passed on into the Great Unseen. God accept him; Christ receive him. I do not think he died in vain.

And Aby did not die in vain. If by his death other men somehow found their resolve to stay and face the front, then his sacrifice, like that of the others, is immeasurable.

Chapter 15

No Time Limit on Justice

Their lives cannot repay us – their death could not undo
The shame that they have laid upon our race
But the slothfulness that wasted and the arrogance that slew,
Shall we leave it unabated in its place?
                                        Rudyard Kipling

When Julian Bickersteth's brother Geoffrey read the letter describing the last hours of young Harry Williams, he was appalled.

> The description of that boy of nineteen's execution in Julian's letter made my blood boil. I think it is the most pathetic thing I have ever read in my life. How can these things be? The irony of a man dying with such magnificent courage after being condemned for cowardice! And the shrieking injustice! How about those Generals who failed their duty at Cambrai – a failure which cost the lives of thousands of brave men? Were they shot? No – given soft billets in England probably. That poor boy's sweetheart! ... Let us remember these things when we talk of the value of war.

The echoes of that shrieking injustice seem not to diminish with the passing of years. In fact, as other nations rehabilitate or pardon their sons who were put to death in similar circumstances, the injustice grows all the more acute and it is difficult to understand the intransigence of successive British governments.

In the tiny French village of Vingré there stands a memorial to six fusiliers who were shot for abandoning their posts. It has stood there

154

since 1925, erected four years after the rehabilitation of the condemned and executed men.

In the year 2000, the five New Zealand soldiers who had been executed were pardoned. The New Zealand Prime Minister, Helen Clark said, 'This announcement will be a relief for the families of the executed soldiers, some of whom have been campaigning for decades to clear the names of the soldiers.'

In 1988, the British government, then Conservative, refused to pardon our servicemen. The opposition was in favour of pardons, but in 1998 when they were in power they refused them, once again showing how pre-election standpoints rarely survive success at the polls. It cannot be said that the Labour government dismissed the appeal for pardons out of hand as it is clear from the statement given to the House by the then Minister for the Armed Forces, Dr John Reid, that considerable effort had been expended. Dr Reid's statement, given on 24 July 1998, was heartfelt and emotional. He had read about a hundred case files of those put before courts martial and shot, and it is clear they had made a profound impression on him. After opening with words about the War in general, he went on:

> For some of our soldiers and their families, however, there has been neither glory nor remembrance. Just over 300 of them died at the hands not of the enemy, but of firing squads from their own side. They were shot at dawn, stigmatised and condemned – a few as cowards, most as deserters. The nature of those deaths and the circumstances surrounding them have long been a matter of contention. Therefore, last May, I said we would look again at their cases.

Dr Reid appraised the House as to the numbers of those convicted of offences that held the death penalty (20,000) and compared these with the numbers actually sentenced to death (over 3,000) and finally with the number whose sentences had been carried into execution and not commuted. He then went on to explain why pardons could not be given.

> However frustrating, the passage of time means that the grounds for a blanket legal pardon on the basis of unsafe conviction just do not exist. We have therefore considered the cases individually.

155

The passage of time is of course a factor. Apart from the court martial files, there is virtually nothing left upon which to judge the cases. Would the same have been true fifty years ago? It is not the fault of those who press for pardons that the details of the cases were kept from the public until the 1990s.

A legal pardon, as envisaged by some, could take one of three forms: a free pardon, a conditional pardon, or a statutory pardon. We have given very serious consideration to this matter. However, the three types of pardon have one thing in common – for each individual case, there must be some concrete evidence for overturning the decision of a legally constituted court, which was charged with examining the evidence in those serious offences.

I have personally examined one third of the records – approximately 100 personal case files. It was a deeply moving experience. Regrettably, many of the records contain little more than the minimum prescribed for this type of court martial – a form recording administrative details and a summary – not a transcript – of the evidence. Sometimes it amounts only to one or two handwritten pages.

I have accepted legal advice that, in the vast majority of cases, there is little to be gleaned from the fragments of the stories that would provide serious grounds for a legal pardon. Eighty years ago, when witnesses were available and the events were fresh in their memories, that might have been a possibility, but the passage of time has rendered it well-nigh impossible in most cases.

Again, whose fault is that, if not successive governments?

So, if we were to pursue the option of formal, legal pardons, the vast majority, if not all, of the cases would be left condemned either by an accident of history which has left us with insufficient evidence to make a judgement, or, even where the evidence is more extensive, by a lack of sufficient evidence to overturn the original verdicts. In short, most would be left condemned, or in some cases re-condemned, 80 years after the event.

I repeat here what I said last May when I announced the review – that we did not wish, by addressing one perceived injustice, to create another. I wish to be fair to all, and, for that reason I do not believe that pursuing possible individual formal legal pardons for a small number, on the basis of impressions from the surviving evidence, will best serve the purpose of justice or the sentiment of Parliament. The point is that now, 80 years after the events and on the basis of the evidence, we cannot distinguish between those who deliberately let down their country and their comrades in arms and those who were not guilty of desertion or cowardice.

This argument is only valid if we consider it right that men and boys could be executed for military offences at all. For pragmatic reasons it may have seemed necessary, but was it right? Some of the men had good records – some outstanding. Some had poor records – some pretty dire. But the men were not shot for their antecedents. The greater question here is, were these men let down by their country, and do we continue to let this injustice stand 'unabated in its place'?

Current knowledge of the psychological effects of war, for example, means that we now accept that some injustices may have occurred. Suspicions cannot be completely allayed by examination of the sparse records. We have therefore decided also to reject the option of those who have urged us to leave well alone and to say nothing. To do nothing, in the circumstances, would be neither compassionate nor humane.

Today, there are four things that we can do in this House, which sanctioned and passed the laws under which these men were executed. First, with the knowledge now available to us, we can express our deep sense of regret at the loss of life. There remain only a very few of our fellow countrymen who have any real understanding or memory of life and death in the trenches and on the battlefields of the first world war. This year marks the 80th anniversary of the end of the war, and we are recalling and remembering the conditions of that war, and all those who endured them, both those who died at the hands of the enemy, and those who were executed. We remember, too, those who did their awful duty in the firing squads.

157

This last sentence is most valid. Those who had to form firing parties were often traumatized by the ordeal. When nearing the end of his long life, Ernest Scully was asked by his daughter what was the worst thing he had ever had to do. Ernest had served in South Africa with the 3rd Infantry and then the 4th Mounted Rifles as a trooper. In 1915 he travelled to England where he received a commission with the 10th Hussars. He recounted his worst experience as having to command a firing party. 'People joined the Army to fight,' he told his daughter. 'Not to shoot a poor frightened boy.'

In the year 2002 a Hertfordshire schoolgirl carried out a poignant duty on behalf of her grandfather. He had formed part of a firing party, and had never forgotten the lad he had to shoot. Two generations after the event, his granddaughter laid a wreath on the grave of the executed soldier.

> Secondly, in our regret, and as we approach a new century, let us remember that pardon implies more than legality and legal formality. Pardon involves understanding, forgiveness, tolerance and wisdom. I trust that hon. Members will agree that, while the passage of time has distanced us from the evidence and the possibility of distinguishing guilt from innocence, and has rendered the formality of pardon impossible, it has also cast great doubt on the stigma of condemnation.

One can almost feel the conflict within Dr Reid. It is almost as if he wants to say that pardons will be allowed, but the exigencies of politics will not allow it. In that he says the formality of pardon is impossible, how can this be? How can it be impossible for Britain in 1998, yet possible for New Zealand two years later? The Queen, being the head of the Commonwealth, was allowed to put her seal on the Act that pardoned the New Zealand soldiers. It appears absurd she cannot be allowed to do the same for the remaining 306 British and Commonwealth servicemen.

> If some men were found wanting, it was not because they all lacked courage, backbone or moral fibre. Among those executed were men who had bravely volunteered to serve their country. Many had given good and loyal service. In a sense, those who were executed were as much victims of the war as the soldiers and airmen who were killed in action, or who died

of wounds or disease, like the civilians killed by aerial or naval bombardment, or like those who were lost at sea. As the 20th century draws to a close, they all deserve to have their sacrifice acknowledged afresh. I ask hon. Members to join me in recognising those who were executed for what they were – the victims, with millions of others, of a cataclysmic and ghastly war.

Thirdly, we hope that others outside the House will recognise all that, and that they will consider allowing the missing names to be added to books of remembrance and war memorials throughout the land.

Finally, there is one other thing that we can do as we look forward to a new millennium. The death penalty is still enshrined in our military law for five offences, including misconduct in action and mutiny. I can tell the House that Defence Ministers will invite Parliament to abolish the death penalty for military offences in the British armed forces in peace and in war.

To this, the Members chorused 'Hear, hear.'

There are deeply held feelings about the executions. Eighty years after those terrible events, we have tried to deal with a sensitive issue as fairly as possible for all those involved. In remembrance of those who died in the war, the poppy fields of Flanders became a symbol for the shattered innocence and the shattered lives of a lost generation. May those who were executed, with the many, many others who were victims of war, finally rest in peace. Let all of us who have inherited the world that followed remember with solemn gratitude, the sacrifices of those who served that we might live in peace.

In the final analysis, Dr Reid has all but pardoned the men, and one cannot help but feel that if it were within his remit, pardons would have been issued. But following his answer to a question put by Mike Hancock, Member for Portsmouth South, one wonders if political rhetoric has dulled our ears.

Mr Hancock questioned the impossibility of issuing formal pardons, and addressed the point of the inability to distinguish those who deserved them from those who did not.

The nation owes it to these men to show the compassion that is needed. Perhaps, just perhaps, some were guilty of the offences in question, but pardoning them all is a price the nation would willingly pay in order, once and for all, to lift this stain from our nation's military history.

Dr Reid's answer hid the real issue behind a premise that to issue pardons would be to throw aside legal precedent and would fly in the face of democracy and all that so many servicemen had fought and died for. It is surprising at this point that business in the House was not concluded, due to the sound of so many of those servicemen spinning in their graves. The argument is absurd. Once again, how can such a different measure of what is legally possible be applied to New Zealand? In his closing words, Dr Reid again tries to take the sting out of the government's refusal to pardon.

> We have expressed regret and the view that – like all those who died – those people were victims of that terrible, terrible war. We have asked that the stigma of the executions be lifted and that those names be added to the books of remembrance and memorials ...
>
> ... I hope – for the benefit of the families and those who were executed – that we can genuinely say, 'Let them rest in peace.'

I suspect that Aby has rested in perfect peace for these many long years since he was shot, shoulder to shoulder and full square with all those who died in that war. His grave only differs from those of the other sixteen men in the ranks of the Final Parade at Labourse in that it bears the Star of David. Of all the soldiers who died before the firing squads, only one grave makes any reference to the fact that it marks the final resting place of one of those 'shot at dawn', and that was at the request of the man's father. It is the grave of Private Albert Ingham. His father chose these words for the headstone:

SHOT AT DAWN
ONE OF THE FIRST TO ENLIST
A WORTHY SON
OF HIS FATHER

The reason why only one of the executed soldiers' graves gives any indication of his fate is explained in a letter from the War Graves Commission dated 12 April 1922.

> It should be explained that the names of the soldiers [executed] are not given in the publication 'Soldiers Died in the Great War'. The Commission however has decided on consideration to erect headstones, of the usual pattern, over their graves without any reference to the manner of their death, or, if their graves are not known, to commemorate them in the same way as the other officers and men where graves are unrecorded.

This was an early indication perhaps, that there was no wish, even at the time, to perpetuate the stigma. But stigma will always remain so long as successive governments withhold the only redress which will expunge it fully and forever. It matters little to Aby whether or not he is pardoned. There is no ghost held earthbound by injustice, waiting Hollywood-like for some final release. If pardons were issued, there would be no collective sigh from the executed men as their spirits shed ethereal bonds and joined their comrades in long overdue rest. So why do pardons matter?

Of course, they matter very much to those few remaining relatives of the soldiers. Children deprived of fathers; younger generations deprived of grandfathers. Aby's niece, never to know but always to feel a loss at never knowing her uncle, and witnessing the pain of Kate, her mother and Aby's sister. Kate would shut herself away every Remembrance Sunday, and it was not until she grew up that Aby's niece knew why.

There is another group to whom the issue of pardons is important. Ironically, it is those people who have faith in our governments to do the right thing, people who care about our laws and our history, those who care most about that commodity which supersedes even laws – and that is justice.

The government has expressed regret, without apology. The government seeks to remove stigma, without issuing pardons. In fairness, they are not the same government who existed eighty years ago. But then neither are they the government who presided over the slave trade, and yet an apology was issued for Britain's part in that cruel and degrading commerce, at a time when dealing in human beings was perfectly legal and even thought by many pious people to be within the bounds of morality.

It is fitting and right that whenever possible we make amends for our mistakes in the past. And lest detractors fear the besmirching of famous names, there is absolutely no necessity to pair apology with blame. Let the generals rest in peace with their laurels intact. They were men of their time, and we cannot know the working of their minds or the experiences that made them who they were. But give Aby his laurels too. He volunteered. He fought. He endured for many months. He suffered the pain of wounds. Should it all be made to count for nothing because one day following many, it all became more than he could bear?

If the British government's apology to the nations that suffered at our hands from the slave trade tells us one thing, it is that there really is no time limit on justice. If that ideal can be applied to events of more than 200 years ago, surely it can be applied to times within the experience of our own grandparents.

For a final word on the subject of pardons, it is fitting to record the words of Andrew MacKinlay, Member of Parliament for Thurrock and champion of the call for pardons.

> My postbag shows beyond all doubt that, in a sense, those men have been pardoned by the highest court in the land – British public opinion.

Epilogue

Is it because the lad is dead
My eyes are doing a double duty,
And drink, for his sake and in his stead,
Twice their accustomed draught of beauty;

Or does the intoxicating Earth
Ferment in me with stronger leaven,
Because, for seeing the year's rebirth,
He loans me eyes that look on heaven?

Frank Sidgwick

Tragically, the Bevistein's home was to receive more bad news before the end of the War. On 21 March 1918 – two years and a day after Aby's death – Alec Kutchinsky was killed while serving with the King's Royal Rifle Corps. Although Alec was four years older than Aby, they had grown up together and for some years attended the same school. The death of so close a family friend must have deepened a wound in the Bevistein family, still raw from Aby's passing.

Rebecca never truly recovered from her son's death, although her grief must have been tempered with some happiness from time to time, such as in May 1921 when Kate got married to a young tailor called Louis Sadick. Louis moved in with the Bevisteins and shared the top floor of their Anthony Street house. The Kutchinskys still lived downstairs and the two families remained firm in their friendship.

Rebecca's health declined, and she died just twelve years after Aby, having suffered for virtually the whole period. Still the family stayed on at Anthony Street. Kate and Louis had children – Aby's nieces – and although space was limited they made do. Joseph attended synagogue and was particular in his observation of religious laws.

Then came another war, and Jews were targeted once more. The bombing of vast areas of the East End was no accident. These bombs were not all strays intended for the docklands. This was made very clear by William Joyce, the leading British fascist who emigrated to Germany and became known as Lord Haw Haw for the upper-crust accent he adopted.

> Hardest of all, the Luftwaffe will smash Stepney. I know the East End! Those dirty Jews and Cockneys will run like rabbits into their holes.

Jane Street was smashed, Fenton Street was flattened, and Anthony Street was completely obliterated. Only short, cobble-stoned stubs of these streets remain today, making abortive, dead-end flights south from the Commercial Road. The Bevisteins and the Kutchinskys relocated to Golders Green and they moved into homes just a few minutes' walk from each other. The blitz had not broken the friendship of the two families.

Unfortunately, Joseph Bevistein, who had lived under the rule of tsars and kings, did not survive to see the peace. He died in 1944. Kate did not enjoy good health, nor was she ever entirely free of the pain of losing her only brother. Each Remembrance Day renewed the wound. She died well before her time, aged just sixty.

Today, Aby's surviving niece remembers the effect of Aby's loss. She remembers his name, for she was robbed of the opportunity of ever knowing him as a person. But his name will be passed down to new generations who carry Joseph's, and therefore Aby's blood, and though the impact he made on his own times was but a whisper in the annals of history, we know more of him than many another from those hard days.

Aby was not a hero. He was an ordinary lad and a soldier whose service was indistinguishable from the hundreds of thousands of others who died, and the millions who served. That being the case, why should we remember his name while we forget those of uncountable others? If for nothing else, then he should be remembered for what was taken from him and what is still withheld: the right for his sacrifice to merge with the sacrifices of the others with a clear and unblemished record.

It is said that a person is not truly dead until there is nobody left to remember him.

Die hard, Aby. Die hard.

Appendix I
Final Parade at Labourse

Such discipline on Parade
Would put to shame a Guard's Brigade:
So long, so rigid, to remain like this
And still no order to dismiss

William Clarke

Those on Final Parade with Aby, in Labourse Communal Cemetery

Rank/No.	Name	Age	Regiment	Comment
2nd Lieutenant	R.P. Davies	31	4th Royal Welsh Fusiliers	Died 5/10/15. Husband of Elizabeth Davies of Bernard Road, Wrexham
L/Sgt 9586	F. Halsey		2nd Bedfordshire Rgmt	Died 26/9/15
L/Cpl 149948	A. Rose	44	9th Leicestershire Rgmt	Died 21/11/16. Husband of Mrs B. Rose of Shepshed, Loughborough
L/Cpl 13386	A.H. Smith		1st Royal Welsh Fusiliers	Died 27/9/15
Pte 11/1799	Abraham Bevistein	17	11th Middlesex Rgmt	Died 20/3/16. Details shown as they are known to be. Details of other soldiers shown as recorded by WGC
Sapper 2186	T. Bray		West Riding Field Coy, RE	Died 29/12/16
Pte S/2196	P.E. Hoad	17	5th Royal Sussex Rgmt	Died 28/7/15. Son of Mrs Sarah Parsons of Ferry Road, Rye, Sussex

Rank/No.	Name	Age	Regiment	Comment
Pte 5/2470	William James Lavender	20	5th Royal Sussex Rgmt	Died 28/7/15. Son of William and Charlotte Lavender, St Leonards-on-Sea
Sapper 42764	J. Lockhart	33	74th Field Coy, RE	Died 24/7/15. Son of James and Jane Lockhart, and husband of Mrs A.E. Lockhart, Warrington
Pte 21161	Harry Martin		9th Essex Rgmt	Died 20/3/16
Pte 1598	M. McDonald		4th Black Watch	Died 6/12/15
Pte 11427	J. Norman		2nd Royal Warwickshire Rgmt	Died 27/9/15
Pte 14036	Harold Teat	18	8th Devonshire Rgmt	Died 26/9/15. Son of John and Agnes Teat, Rochdale
Pte 7547	William Landreth Thompson	27	6th Buffs	Died 22/4/16. Son of Mary and Moses Thompson. Husband of Florence Rosetta Hedley, Newcastle-on-Tyne
Driver 46164	Wilfred Ward	22	74th Field Coy, RE	Died 24/7/15. Son of Stephen and Annie Ward. Born Scorton, Yorks
Pte 15231	H.C. Weston		2nd Bedfordshire Rgmt	Died 27/9/15
Pte 10916	A. Wood		1st Scots Guards	Died 10/7/15

Appendix II

Goodbye, the Old Battalion

A letter from Lieutenant General, Adjutant General to the Forces, to the Lord Mayor of London, 30 November 1918, tells what became of Aby's battalion.

My Lord

I forward the following brief statement of the services rendered to the country during the present hostilities by the 11th (Service) Battalion, The Duke of Cambridge's Own (Middlesex Regiment) feeling sure that it will be of great interest to you and to all those connected with the Regiment.

The recent re-organization of Infantry in France involved the disbandment of certain Battalions amongst which is the 11th (Service) Battalion, The Duke of Cambridge's Own (Middlesex Regiment).

The Battalion was formed on the 26th August 1914, and after training in England the battalion left Aldershot for France on May 31st 1915, landed at Boulogne June 1st and proceeded to the Armentieres area for instruction in trench warfare being attached to its own 1st Battalion.

It was in this area till the end of September, carrying out some successful bombing raids. On September 30th it took over part of the German positions captured North East of Vermelles and assisted to consolidate and hold these against German counter attacks.

It remained in this neighbourhood for the last three months of 1915 and first half of 1916, repeating an attack near the Quarries on February 13th for which it was specially congratulated by the General Officer Commanding, First Army, and carrying out several minor operations, including a very successful raid on February 29th.

In July it moved to the Somme, attacked near Ovillers July 3rd–7th, taking two objectives and was again engaged near Pozieres (end of July) and near Flers and Guedecourt (October). It received 11 M.Ms.

It remained in the Somme area till February 1917 when it took over part of the Arras sector and carried out a very successful daylight raid.

In the battle East of Arras on April 9th the battalion was successful in gaining its objectives, immediately East of Arras and South of the Scarpe it was subsequently in severe fighting round Monchy Le Freux (May 3rd and 12th) and gained an M.C. and eight M.Ms.

After remaining in the Monchy area all the summer it moved to Gonnelieu for the great attack of November 20th. In this it distinguished itself by taking over 150 prisoners. It was in action again on November 25th and in the German counter attack of November 30th.

Later it moved to the Fleurbaix area and was there when disbanded on February 6th 1918 the largest party of its officers went to the 4th Battalion, other drafts being sent to the 1st, 7th (T.F.) and the 8th (T.F.) Battalions.

In every engagement in which this Battalion took part it upheld the brilliant and glorious traditions of the Duke of Cambridge's Own (Middlesex Regiment) to which it belonged.

Battalions of this Regiment have served in all quarters of the globe and have taken part in such historic battles as:- Mysore, Seringapatam, Albuhera, Ciudad Rodrigo, Badajoz, Vittoria, Pyrenees, Nivelle, Nive, Peninsula, Alma, Inkerman, Sevastopol and in the campaigns in New Zealand, South Africa 1879, and South Africa 1900–02 taking part in the Relief of Ladysmith.

Although the 11th Battalion has been disbanded the Officers, Warrant Officers, Non-Commissioned Officers and the men have not been lost to the Middlesex Regiment; they have all been drafted into other Battalions of the Middlesex Regiment and will continue to uphold the name and traditions of this Regiment with the same spirit, loyalty and esprit-de-corps as they have done in the 11th (Service) Battalion.

> I have the honour to be,
> Your most obedient and humble Servant,

Lieut-General
Adjutant General to the Forces.

Sources and Bibliography

Published Sources

Adler, Rev. M., *British Jewry Book of Honour, 1914–1918*, Selous Books.

Ayscough, J, *French Windows: Experiences of a Chaplain at the Front*, Arnold, 1917.

Babington, Anthony, *For the Sake of Example*, Penguin Books, 2002.

Bickersteth, E., *Bickersteth Diaries*, Leo Cooper (Pen & Sword Books).

Birmingham, G.A., *With a Padre in France*, Hodder and Stoughton, 1918.

Blackburn, H.W., *This Also Happened on the Western Front*, Hodder and Stoughton, 1932.

Brown, Malcolm, *The Western Front*, Pan Books, 2001.

Brown, Malcolm, *Tommy Goes to War*, Tempus Publishing, 2001.

Bull, Dr Stephen, *World War I Trench Warfare (1)*, Osprey Publishing, 2002.

Chappell, Mike, *British Battle Insignia (1) 1914–18*, Osprey Publishing, 1986.

Chappell, Mike, *The British Army in World War I (1)*, Osprey Publishing, 2003.

Cohen, Abraham, *Everyman's Talmud*, Schocken Books.

Coppard, George, *With a Machine Gun to Cambrai*, Cassell Military Paperbacks, 1999.

Corns, C. and Hughes-Wilson, J., *Blindfold and Alone*, Cassell, 2001.

Corrigan, Gordon, *Mud, Blood and Poppycock*, Cassell, 2003.

Dunn, Captain J.C., *The War the Infantry Knew 1914–1919*, Abacus History, 1994.

Gartner, Lloyd P., *The Jewish Immigrant in England, 1870 to 1914*, Vallentine Mitchell, 2001.

Hay, Ian, *The First Hundred Thousand*, Isis Publishing, 2000.

Holt, Tonie and Valmai, *My Boy Jack*, Leo Cooper (Pen & Sword Books), 1998.

Houseman, A.E., *The Works of A.E. Houseman*, Wordsworth Poetry Library, 1994.

Johnstone, W. and A.K., *The World Wide Atlas*, W. and A.K. Johnstone.

Keesee, D.M., *Too Young to Die: Boy Soldiers of the Union Army 1861 to 1865*, Blue Acorn Press, 2001.

London, Jack, *The People of the Abyss*, Lawrence Hill Books, 1995.

Manning, Frederic, *Her Privates We*, Serpent's Tail, first published 1930.

Middleton-Brumwell, P., *The History of the 12th (Eastern) Division in the Great War, 1914–1918*, The Naval and Military Press, first published 1923.

Moore, William, *The Thin Yellow Line*, Leo Cooper (Pen & Sword Books), 1974.

Oram, Gerard, *Worthless Men*, Francis Boutle Publishers, 1998.

Owen, Wilfred, *The Collected Poems of Wilfred Owen*, Chatto and Windus, 1963.

Pankhurst, Sylvia, *The Home Front*, Hutchinson, 1933.

Parsons, I.M., ed., *Men Who March Away*, Book Club Associates, 1978.

Pearce, Cyril, *Comrades in Conscience*, Francis Boutle Publishers, 2001.

Pegler, Martin, *British Tommy 1914–18*, Osprey Publishing, 1999.

Putkowski, Julian and Sykes, Julian, *Shot at Dawn*, Pen & Sword Books, 1989.

Rawson, Andrew, *Loos-Hohenzollern: French Flanders*, Pen & Sword Books.

Rosen, Harold, *Are You Still Circumcised?*, Five Leaves Publications.

Sellers, Leonard, *Death for Desertion*, Pen & Sword Books, 2003.

Sheridan, Yoel, *From Here to Obscurity*, Tenterbooks, 2001.

Steuart, R.H.J., *March, Kind Comrade*, Sheed and Ward.

Tiplady, T., *The Cross at the Front*, Epworth, 1939.

Warner, Philip, *The Battle of Loos*, Wordsworth Military Library, 1976.

Weintraub, Stanley, *Silent Night*, Simon and Schuster, 2001.

Westlake, Ray, *Kitchener's Army*, Spellmount, 1989.

Wyrall, Everard, *The Die-Hards in the Great War*, The Naval and Military Press.

Yrondy, Pierre, *Les Fusilles de Vingré*, L'Oiseau de Minerve, 1999.

Maps

IGN Serie Bleur, *Aire-Sur-La-Lys*, Map No. 2304E
IGN Serie Bleur, *Bethune*, Map No. 2405O
IGN Serie Bleur, *Liller*, Map No. 2305E

Archive Sources

Commonwealth War Graves Commission (CWGC)
British Newspaper Library, Colindale (Bcol)
Family Records Office (FRO)
Imperial War Museum (IWM)
London Metropolitan Archives (LMA)
Public Record Office (PRO)
Special Collection, Southampton University (SC)

CWGC   Personal details of fallen Middlesex men quoted in *Die Hard, Aby!*

Bcol   *The Women's Dreadnoght*, Vol. III, No. 5, Saturday, 22 April 1916.

FRO   Death and marriage certificates of members of the Bevistein and Kutchinsky families.
1901 Census.

LMA   Lower Chapman Street School Register (XO95/025)
         Aby's entry (LCC/EO/DIV5 LOW/A+D/6, Folio 1053)
         Alec Kutchinsky's entry (as above, Folio 330)
         Kate's entry (as above, Girls Register, Folio 28)
    Lower Chapman Street School Log Book (LCC/EO/DIV5/LOW/LB/1-3)
    Map. St George's-in-the-East, North Ward, OS Lon 25 inch, 1916.

PRO   Harry Martin's Case File. WO71/455
    Aby's Court Martial Case File. WO71/456
    William Thompson's Case File. WO71/460
    Henry Carter's Case File. WO71/461
    Harry William's Case File. WO71/627

Letters from War Graves Commission. WO93/49

War Diary of 11th Middlesex. WO95/1856
War Diary of 38th Field Ambulance. WO95/1844

Captain A. Redford. Personal File. WO339/213
Lt. Harry Hughes-Jones Personal File. WO339/11440
Lt. T.L. Mills Personal File. WO339/7995
Lt. E.R. Scully Personal File. WO339/44924
Captain The Rev. C.C.T. Naters' Personal File. WO374/50039

SC   Adler, Rev. M.; Four appointment diaries. MS 125

Other Sources

First World War Website: www.firstworldwar.com
Hayman, J., *Jews in Britain During the Great War 1914–1918*, Manchester University.
Hellfire Corner Website: www.hellfire-corner.demon.co.uk
Information concerning SS *Batavier III* and SS *Princess Victoria*: www.theshipslist.com
Newman, A., *Trains, Ships and Shelters*, University of Leicester, Occasional Papers.

Index

Index